FACING THE CHAIR

A Da Capo Press Reprint Series

CIVIL LIBERTIES IN AMERICAN HISTORY

GENERAL EDITOR: LEONARD W. LEVY

Brandeis University

FACING THE CHAIR

STORY OF THE AMERICANIZATION
OF TWO FOREIGNBORN WORKMEN

by

JOHN DOS PASSOS

DA CAPO PRESS · NEW YORK · 1970

A Da Capo Press Reprint Edition

This Da Capo Press edition of
Facing the Chair is an unabridged
republication of the first edition published
in Boston in 1927.

Library of Congress Catalog Card Number 72-104066
SBN 306-71871-5

Published by Da Capo Press
A Division of Plenum Publishing Corporation
227 West 17th Street, New York, N. Y. 10011

Manufactured in the United States of America

FACING THE CHAIR

STORY OF THE AMERICANIZATION
OF TWO FOREIGNBORN WORKMEN

by

JOHN DOS PASSOS

PUBLISHED BY
SACCO-VANZETTI DEFENSE COMMITTEE
BOSTON. MASS.
1927

"AND I WILL SAY TO YOUR HONOR THAT A GOVERNMENT THAT HAS COME TO HONOR ITS OWN SECRETS MORE THAN THE LIVES OF ITS CITIZENS HAS BECOME A TYRANNY WHETHER YOU CALL IT A REPUBLIC, A MONARCHY OR ANYTHING ELSE."

—from Atty. William G. Thompson's argument before Judge Thayer, pleading for a new trial.

ANATOLE FRANCE'S APPEAL TO THE AMERICAN PEOPLE

—————————

October 31, 1921

People of United States of America,

Listen to the appeal of an old man of the old world who is not a foreigner, for he is the fellow citizen of all mankind.

In one of your states two men, Sacco and Vanzetti, have been convicted for a crime of opinion.

It is horrible to think that human beings should pay with their lives for the exercise of that most sacred right which, no matter what party we belong to, we must all defend.

Don't let this most iniquitous sentence be carried out.

The death of Sacco and Vanzetti will make martyrs of them and cover you with shame.

You are a great people. You ought to be a just people. There are crowds of intelligent men among you, men who think. I prefer to appeal to them. I say to them beware of making martyrs. That is the unforgivable crime that nothing can wipe out and that weighs on generation after generation.

Save Sacco and Vanzetti.

Save them for your honor, for the honor of your children, and for the generations yet unborn.

ANATOLE FRANCE.

EUGENE V. DEBS TO THE WORKERS OF AMERICA

Gene Debs is dead.   Gene Debs lives in the hearts and minds of millions of Americans.   This is his last appeal for justice.

The supreme court of Massachusetts has spoken at last and Bartolomeo Vanzetti and Nicola Sacco, two of the bravest and best scouts that ever served the labor movement, must go to the electric chair.

The decision of this capitalist judicial tribunal is not surprising.   It accords perfectly with the tragical farce and the farcical tragedy of the entire trial of these two absolutely innocent and shamefully persecuted working men.

The evidence at the trial in which they were charged with a murder they had no more to do with committing than I had, would have convicted no one but a "foreign labor agitator" in the hydrophobic madness of the world war.   In any other case the perjured and flagrantly made-to-order testimony, repeatedly exposed and well known to the court, would have resulted in instantaneous acquittal.   Not even a sheep-killing dog but only a "vicious foreign-radical" could have been convicted under such shameless evidence.

Sacco and Vanzetti were framed and doomed from the start. Not all the testimony that could have been piled up to establish their innocence beyond a question of doubt could have saved them in that court.   The trial judge was set and immovable.   There must be a conviction.   It was so ordained by the capitalist powers that be, and it had to come.   And there must be no new trial granted lest the satanic perjury of the testimony and the utter rottenness of the proceedings appear too notoriously rank and revolting in spite of the conspiracy of the press to keep the public in ignorance of the disgraceful and damaging facts.

Aside from the disgustingly farcical nature of the trial which could and should have ended in fifteen minutes in that master-class court, the refined malice and barbaric cruelty of these capitalist tribunals, high and low, may read in the insufferable torture inflicted thru six long, agonizing years upon their imprisoned and helpless victims.

It would have been merciful to the last degree in comparison had they been boiled in oil, burned at the stake, or had every joint torn from their bodies on the wheel when they were first seized as prey to glut the vengeance of slave drivers, who wax fat and savage in child labor and who never forgive an "agitator" who is too rigidly honest to be bribed, too courageous to be intimidated, and too defiant to be suppressed.

And that is precisely why the mill-owning, labor-sweating malefactors of Massachusetts had Sacco and Vanzetti framed, pounced upon, thrown into a dungeon, and sentenced to be murdered by their judicial and other official underlings.

I appeal to the working men and women of America to think of these two loyal comrades, these two honest, clean-hearted brothers of ours, in this fateful hour in which they stand face to face with their bitter and ignominious doom.

The capitalist courts of Massachusetts have had them on the rack day and night, devouring the flesh of their bodies and torturing their souls for six long years to finally deal the last vicious, heartless blow, aimed to send them to their graves as red-handed felons and murderers.

Would that it were in my power to make that trial judge and those cold-blooded gowns in the higher court suffer for just one day the agonizing torture, the pitiless misery, the relentless cruelty they have inflicted in their stony-hearted "judicial calmness and serenity" upon Sacco and Vanzetti thru six endless years!

Perhaps some day these solemn and begowned servants of the ruling powers may have to atone for their revolting crime against innocence in the name of justice!

They have pronounced the doom of their long suffering victims and the press declares that the last word has been spoken. I deny it.

There is another voice yet to be heard and that is the voice of an outraged working class. It is for labor now to speak and for the labor movement to announce its decision, and that decision is and must be, SACCO AND VANZETTI ARE INNOCENT AND SHALL NOT DIE!

To allow these two intrepid proletarian leaders to perish as red-handed criminals would forever disgrace the cause of labor in the United States. The countless children of generations yet to come would blush for their sires and grand sires and never forgive their cowardice and poltroonery.

It cannot be possible, and I shall not think it possible, that the American workers will desert, betray and deliver to their executioner two men who have stood as staunchly true, as unflinchingly loyal in the cause of labor as have Sacco and

Vanzetti, whose doom has been pronounced by the implacable enemies of the working class.

Now is the time for all labor to be aroused and to rally as one vast host to vindicate its assailed honor, to assert its self-respect, and to issue its demand that in spite of the capitalist-controlled courts of Massachusetts honest and innocent working-men whose only crime is their innocence of crime and their loyalty to labor, shall not be murdered by the official hirelings of the corporate powers that rule and tyrannize over the state.

It does not matter what the occupation of the worker may be, what he is in theory of belief, what union or party he belongs to, this is the supreme cause of us all and the call comes to each of us and to all of us to unite from coast to coast in every state and thruout the whole country to protest in thunder tones against the consummation of that foul and damning crime against labor in the once proud state of Massachusetts.

A thousand protest meetings should be called at once and ring with denunciation of the impending crime.

A milion letters of indignant resentment should roll in on the governor of Massachusetts and upon members of the house of representatives and the senate of the United States.

It is this, and this alone, that will save Sacco and Vanzetti. We cannot ignore this duty to ourselves, to our martyr comrades, to our cause, to justice and humanity without being guilty of treason to our own manhood and outraging our own souls.

Arouse ye toiling millions of the nation and swear by all you hold sacred in the cause of labor and in the cause of truth and justice and all things of good report, that Sacco and Vanzetti, your brothers and mine, innocent as we are, shall not be foully murdered to glut the vengeance of a gang of plutocratic slave drivers!

"WHEN KATZMANN ASKED ME WHAT
I THOUGHT OF SACCO AS A PARTICIP-
ANT IN THE BRAINTREE HOLDUP, I
EXPLAINED TO HIM THAT ANARCH-
ISTS DO NOT COMMIT CRIMES FOR
MONEY BUT FOR A PRINCIPLE, AND
THAT BANDITRY WAS NOT IN THEIR
CODE".

*—from a letter dated Chicago, Ill.
September 29th written by Feri Felix
Weiss to the editor of the Boston
Globe, published with an accompany-
ing affidavit in the New York World,
October 13, 1926.*

AMERICAN FEDERATION OF LABOR
DEMANDS INVESTIGATION

On October 11th, 1926, the American Federation of Labor Convention in Detroit, representing millions of working men passed the following resolution proposing that the American Federation of Labor demand an investigation of the activities of agents of the Department of Justice in the Sacco-Vanzetti case.

Resolution No. 74.—By Delegate Samuel Squibb, International Granite Cutters' Union.

WHEREAS, The case of Sacco and Vanzetti has again come before the public; and

WHEREAS, After six years of imprisonment those who take an interest in this case are now more convinced than ever that Sacco and Vanzetti are not guilty of the crime they were charged with and convicted for; and

WHEREAS, The motion for a new trial based on newly discovered evidence, primarily on the confession of Celestino F. Madeiros, is now before the court of Massachusetts; and

WHEREAS, On this motion for a new trial, affidavits of former agents of the Department of Justice of the United States have been produced that show that there are records on file in the office of the Department of Justice, establishing the fact that there was collaboration between the Department of Justice and the District Attorney of Norfolk County to convict Sacco and Vanzetti on charges of a crime, of which the Department of Justice did not believe them guilty; and

WHEREAS, The Attorney General has refused access to the records in the case to the Counsel for the Defense, in spite of his urgent request for the same; and

WHEREAS, A large number of the International Unions affiliated with the American Federation of Labor are deeply interested in the case of Sacco and Vanzetti and have by resolutions adopted at their conventions, expressed the sentiment of their members on this matter; be it, therefore

RESOLVED, That the American Federation of Labor in convention assembled demand an immediate investigation by the Congress of the United States of the actions of the agents of the Department of Justice; the connection of Department of Justice with the conviction of Sacco and Vanzetti; and the refusal of the Department of Justice to disclose its files on the Sacco and Vanzetti case; be it further

RESOLVED, That copies of this resolution be sent to the President and Congress of the United States.

The convention of the American Federation of Labor of last year and of several years prior thereto have repeatedly declared that Sacco and Vanzetti should be accorded a new trial in order that no man's life may be placed in jeopardy without a just and fair trial and be found guilty beyond a reasonable doubt. This insistence for a new trial was predicated on the doubt of many as to the guilt of these men and because of the belief that the enforcement of this decision without a retrial and a full and complete opportunity to present all possible evidence having come to light either as to the guilt or innocence of these men would be a miscarriage of justice.

The resolution presented indicates or at least raises a doubt that evidence has been or is being witheld by the Department of Justice relating to the guilt or innocence of these men. This in itself places the Department of Justice into serious question. It adds further doubt as to the guilt or innocence of the men charged and found guilty of crime. Regardless of the character or attitude of mind of these men toward our government or its institutions as a people we are deeply concerned that the power of government, or that of any of its departments shall at no time be used unconstitutionally to jeopardize the life and liberty of any person. And because of the serious charge thus made we recommend reaffirmation of our former demand for a retrial and reference of this resolution to the Executive Council, with directions that it proceed immediately to inquire into the charge made and to have determined the truth or falsity of this charge by Congressional investigation, if that be necessary.

The report of the committee was adopted by unanimous vote.

"The department of Justice in Boston was anxious to get sufficient evidence against Sacco and Vanzetti to deport them but never succeeded in getting the kind and amount of evidence required for that purpose. It was the opinion of the department agents here that a conviction of Sacco and Vanzetti for murder would be one way of disposing of the two men. It was also the general opinion of such of the agents in Boston as had any actual knowledge of the Sacco-Vanzetti case; that Sacco and Vanzetti, although anarchists and agitators, were not highway robbers and had nothing to do with the South Braintree crime. My opinion and the opinion of most of the older men in the government service, has always been that the South Braintree crime was the work of professionals."

> —*from the affidavit of Lawrence Letherman, July* 8, 1926.

"By calling these men anarchists, I do not mean necessarily that they were inclined to violence, nor do I understand all the different meanings different people would attach to the word 'anarchists.' What I mean is I think they did not believe in organized government or in private property, But I am also thoroughly convinced and always have been, and I believe that is the opinion and always has been the opinion of such Boston agents of the Department of Justice as had any knowledge on the subject, that these men had nothing whatever to do with the South Braintree murders, and that their conviction was the result of cooperation between the Boston agents of the Department of Justice and the District Attorney. It was the general opinion of the Boston agents of the Department of Justice having knowledge of the affair that the South Braintree crime was committed by a gang of professional highwaymen."

—*from the affidavit of Fred J. Weyand, Boston, July 1, 1926.*

FACING THE CHAIR

The evening of May 5th, 1920, Nicola Sacco, an Italian, working as edger in a shoe factory, and Bartolomeo Vanzetti, also an Italian, a fishpeddler, were arrested in a streetcar in Brockton, Massachusetts. The two men were known as radicals and were active in Italian working class organizations in the vicinity of Boston. In Sacco's pocket at the time of his arrest was a draft of a handbill calling a meeting to protest against the illegal imprisonment and possible murder of Salsedo by agents of the Department of Justice. Salsedo was the anarchist printer whose body was found smashed on the pavement of Park Row under the windows of the New York offices of the Department of Justice, where he and his friend Elia had been held without warrant for eight weeks of the third degree. Sacco and Vanzetti were armed when arrested and lied when questioned about their friends and associates. It came out later that they had been trying to get the Overland car of a man named Boda out of a garage in order to go about the country to their friends' houses warning them of a new series of red raids they had been tipped off to expect. At the same time they were collecting radical newspapers and any literature that might seem suspicious to the police. They were arrested, because the garage-owner phoned the police, having been warned to notify them of the movements of any Italians who owned automobiles.

A couple of weeks before, the afternoon of April 15, a peculiarly impudent and brutal crime had been committed in South Braintree, a nearby town, the climax of a long series of holdups and burglaries. Bandits after shooting down a paymaster and his guard in the center of the town had escaped in a Buick touring car with over fifteen thousand dollars in cash. It was generally rumored that the bandits were most of them

Italians. The police had made a great fuss but found no clue to the identity of the murderers. Public feeling was bitter and critical. A victim had to be found. To prove the murderers to have been reds would please everybody. So first Vanzetti was taken over to Plymouth and tried as one of the men who had attempted to hold up a paytruck in Bridgewater early in the morning of the previous Christmas Eve. He was convicted and sentenced to fifteen years imprisonment. Plymouth is owned by the largest cordage works in the world. Several years before Vanzetti had been active in a successful strike against the Cordage. Then he was taken to Dedham and tried with Sacco for the murder of the paymaster and his guard killed in South Braintree. After a stormy trial they were convicted of murder in the first degree. Since then sentence has been stayed by a series of motions for a new trial. One appeal to the Supreme Judicial Court of Massachusetts has been refused and another is pending.

The most important evidence that has come up in the course of the motions is the series of affidavits procured by the defense, proving, as the labor press has always claimed, that operatives of the Department of Justice were active in the trial, and lacking evidence on which to deport Sacco and Vanzetti as radicals, helped in the frameup by which they were convicted as murderers.

"They were bad actors anyway and got what was coming to them," one detective is quoted as saying. That means that any man who gives up his life to the hope of humanizing the treadmill of industry is a bad actor in the minds of the governing class and governing class police. Sacco and Vanzetti are not the only men who have been framed, but they have become symbols. All over the world people are hopefully, heartbrokenly watching the Sacco-Vanzetti Case as a focus in the unending fight for human rights of oppressed individuals and masses against oppressing individuals and masses.

I

WHERE THE CASE STANDS TODAY

On October 23rd 1926 Judge Webster Thayer handed down his decision on the latest motions for a new trial, argued by the defense during the week of September 13th.   The decision is a document of something more than thirty thousand words in length.   A reader unskilled in the technique of legal judgment gets the impression that the document is more of a personal apologium and defense on the part of the court than the impartial decision of a judge.   Not a spark of scientific spirit, or of the consciousness of the infinite possibilities of human error has edged its way into those long involved sentences.

The confession of Madeiros and the elaborate circumstantial case evolved from it by the defense, tending to prove that the South Braintree holdup was committed by members of the Morelli gang of Providence, is dismissed with the following statement:

In conclusion, in so far as the Madeiros affidavit is concerned, it would have been an easy task for this court to transfer the responsibility upon another jury, but if this were done it would be the shirking of a solemn duty that the law places upon the trial court.   Guided by this solemn duty I have examined and studied for several weeks without interruption, the record of the testimony upon this motion and upon the Madeiros deposition; and being controlled only by judgment, reason, and conscience, and after giving as favorable consideration to these defendants as may be consistent with a due regard for the rights of the public and sound principles of law, I am forced to the conclusion that the affidavit of Madeiros is unreliable, untrustworthy and untrue.   To set aside the verdict of a jury affirmed by the Supreme Judicial Court of this commonwealth on such an affidavit would be a mockery upon truth and justice.   Therefore, exercising every right vested in this court in the granting of motions for new trials by the law of this commonwealth, the motion for a new trial is hereby denied.

Further on in this comment upon the plea that Department
of Justice agents worked with the prosecution to obtain conviction for murder against Sacco and Vanzetti although they
considered them to be innocent (based on the now famous
affidavits of Letherman and Weyand):

Cases cannot be decided on the ground of public opinion, but
upon reason, judgment, and in accordance with law; for cases
cannot be decided on mystery, suspicion or propaganda but upon
the actual evidence that is introduced at the trial.   If this were
otherwise God help the poor defendants in criminal cases, if they
are to be acquitted and convicted, not upon evidence and the
law, but upon public opinion, which might be formed as the
result of an unwarranted public opinion or propaganda.

This might seem to the unlegal mind of a man smoking a
cigar at a street corner, a knife that cuts two ways.   To continue
further on:

Have Attorney General Sargent of the United States and his
subordinates and former Attorney General Palmer under the
administration of President Wilson (for most of the correspondence took place under President Wilson's administration)
stooped so low and are they so degraded that they were willing,
by the concealment of evidence to enter into a fraudulent
conspiracy with the government of Massachusetts to send two
men to the electric chair, not because they were murderers, but
because they were radicals?

Judge Thayer answers, No.   But will that be the verdict
of fairminded men and women when the full truth of this case
is known?   Will that be the verdict of workingmen the world
over who see their own image in Sacco and Vanzetti?   In the face
of the evidence as it stands would a plain mind, free from legal
technicalities and sectional bitterness answers No?
This decision leaves one more chance of appeal to the
Supreme Judicial Court before sentence, but as that court makes
decisions only on points of law and not on the human merits of
a case, the hope of reversal is slim.   After that the only appeal
is to executive clemency, or to the Supreme Court of the United
States on the plea that the defendants were convicted without due
process of law.   A pretty forlorn hope.

Sacco and Vanzetti are not asking for pardon, they are asking for justice. Remember that when it became evident that Tom Mooney was innocent of the Preparedness Parade bombing for which he had been convicted in California, instead of his being freed, his sentence was commuted to life. He is still in jail a victim of executive clemency.

Sacco and Vanzetti want justice, not clemency.

Only an immense surge of protest from all classes and conditions of men can save them from the Chair.

II

THE HEARING OF THE SEVENTH MOTION

Another hearing of a motion for a new trial. Six have been denied so far. Sacco and Vanzetti have been six years in jail. This time there are no guards with riotguns, no state troopers riding round the courthouse. No excitement of any sort. Everyone has forgotten the great days of the Red Conspiracy, the passion to sustain law and order against the wave of radicalism, against foreigners, and the 'moral rats gnawing at the foundations of the commonwealth' that Attorney-General Palmer spoke of so eloquently. In this court there are no prisoners in a cage, no hysterical witnesses, no credulous jury under the sign of the screaming eagle. Quiet, dignity; almost like a class in a lawschool. The case has been abstracted into a sort of mathematics. Only the lawyers for the defense and for the prosecution, Ranney from the District Attorney's office, Thompson and Ehrmann for the defense, two small tables of newspaper men, on the benches a few Italians, some professional liberals and radicals, plainclothes men with rumpsteak faces occupying the end seats.

The court attendants make everybody get up. The Judge comes in on the heels of a man in a blue uniform. Judge Thayer is a very small man with a little grey lined shingle face, nose glasses tilting out at the top across a sudden little hawknose. He walks with a firm bustling tread. The black gown that gives him the power of life and death (the gown of majesty of

the blind goddess the law) sticks out a little behind.   Another
attendant walks after him.   The judge climbs up to his high
square desk.   The judge speaks.   His voice crackles dryly as
old papers.

Affidavits, affidavits read alternately by counsel in the
stillness of the yellowvarnished courtroom.   Gradually as the
reading goes on the courtroom shrinks.   Tragic figures of men
and women grow huge like shadows cast by a lantern on a wall;
the courtroom becomes a tiny pinhole through which to see a
world of huge trampling forces in conflict.

First it's the story of the life of Celestino Madeiros, a poor
Portuguese boy brought up in New Bedford.   He learned
Americanism all right, he suffered from no encumbering ideas
of social progress; the law of dawg eat dawg was morbidly vivid
in his mind from the first.   Hardly out of school he was up in
court for 'breaking and entering'.   No protests from him about
the war.   He and his sister and another man dressed up in
uniform and collected money for some vaguely phoney patriotic
society, The American Rescue League.   By the spring of 1920
he was deep in the criminal world that is such an apt cartoon
of the world of legitimate business.   He was making good.   He
was in with the Morelli brothers of Providence, a gang of
freight-car robbers, bootleggers, pimps, hijackers and miscellaneous thugs.   The great wave of highway robbery that followed
the war was at its height.   For three years the leaders of
society had been proclaiming the worthlessness of human life.
Is it surprising that criminals should begin to take them at their
word?

Scared to death, blind drunk, Madeiros, an overgrown boy
of eighteen, was in the back seat of the Buick touring car that
carried off the tragic holdup outside the Rice and Hutchins
shoefactory at South Braintree. Probably on his share of the
payroll he went south, once he got out of the Rhode Island jail
where another episode of breaking and entering had landed
him.   He came back north with his money spent and worked
as a bouncer at the Bluebird Inn, a 'disorderly' road house at
Seekonk, Mass. and fell at last into the clutches of the
Massachusetts law through a miserable failure to duplicate the

daring South Braintree holdup at Wrentham, where he shot an aged bank cashier and ran without trying to get any loot.   At his trial he sat so hunched and motionless that he seemed an imbecile.   Not even when his mother threw an epileptic fit in the courtroom and was carried out rigid and foaming did he look up.   At the Dedham jail he was put in the cell next to Sacco. He could see Sacco going out to meet his wife and kids when they came to see him.   The idea of an innocent man going to the chair worried him.   For him everything had crashed.   It had been on his own confession that he had been convicted of the Wrentham murder.   He seems to have puzzled for a long time to find some way of clearing Sacco and Vanzetti without inculpating his old associates, even though he had fallen out with them long ago.   He tried to tell Sacco about it in the jail bathroom, but Sacco, seeing Department of Justice spies everywhere—and with good reason— wouldn't listen to him.   So at last he sent the warden a written confession asking him to forward it to the *Boston American*.   Nothing happened.   The warden kept his mouth shut.   Eventually he sent a new confession to Sacco enclosed in a magazine, begging him to let his lawyer see it.   *"I hereby confess to being in the South Braintree Shoe Company crime and Sacco and Vanzetti were not in said crime.*—CELESTINO F. MADEIROS".

Here is Madeiros's own account of the crime:

On April 15, 1920, I was picked up about 4 A. M. at my boarding house, 181 North Main St., Providence, by four Italians who came in a Hudson five-passenger open touring car. My sister's landlord lived at the same place.   She was then a widow and her name was Mary Bover.   She has since been married, and now lives at 735 Bellville Avenue, New Bedford. There was also living there at the same time a man named Arthur Tatro, who afterwards committed suicide in the house of Correction of New Bedford.   He was Captain and I was Lieutenant in the American Rescue League at that time.   Two or three privates in the league also lived there, whose names I do not remember.

We went from Providence to Randolph, where we changed to a Buick car brought there by another Italian.   We left the Hudson car in the woods and took it again after we did the job, leaving the Buick in the woods in charge of one man, who drove it off to another part of the woods, as I understood.

After we did the job at South Braintree and changed back into the Hudson car at Randolph, we drove very fast through Randolph, and were seen by a boy named Thomas and his sister. His father lives on a street that I think is called Prang Street, and is in the window metal business or something of that kind. I became acquainted with him four years later when I went to live in Randolph with Weeks on the same street. Thomas told me one day in conversation that he saw the car that did the South Braintree job going through Randolph very fast.

When we started we went from Providence first to Boston and then back to Providence, and then back to South Braintree, getting there about noon. We spent some time in a "speak easy" in South Braintree two or three miles from the place of the crime, leaving the car in the yard of the house.

When we went to Boston we went to South Boston and stopped in Andrews Square. I stayed in the car. The others went in a saloon to get information, as they told me, about the money that was to be sent to South Braintree.

I had never been to South Braintree before. These four men persuaded me to go with them two or three nights before when I was talking with them in a saloon in Providence. The saloon was also a pool-room, near my boarding house. They talked like professionals. They said they had done lots of jobs of this kind. They had been engaged in robbing freight cars in Providence. Two were young men from 20 to 25 years old, one was about 40, the other about 35. All wore caps. I then was 18 year old. I do not remember whether they were shaved or not. Two of them did the shooting—the oldest one and another. They were left on the street. The arrangement was that they should meet me in a Providence saloon the next night to divide the money. I went there but they did not come.

I sat on the back seat of the automobile. I had a Colt 38 calibre automatic but did not use it. I was told that I was there to help hold back the crowd in case they made a rush. The curtains on the car were flapping. I do not remember whether there was any shotgun or rifle in the car or not.

These men talked a lot of New York. As soon as I got enough money I went to New York and also Chicago hoping to find them in cabarets spending the money, but I never found them.

They had been stealing silk, shoes, cotton, etc., from freight cars sending it to New York. Two of them lived on South Main

Street and two on North Main Street, in lodging houses. I had known them three months or four.

The old man was called Mike. Another one was called William or Bill. I don't remember what the others were called.

The money that they took from the men in South Braintree was in a black bag, I think.

I was scared to death when I heard the shooting begin.

Both cars had Massachusetts numbers.

The names of these men don't amount to anything. They change them whenever they want to. When they are driven out of New York they come to Providence. I haven't any idea where they are now. I have never seen any of them since.

Sacco and Vanzetti had nothing to do with this job, and neither did Gerald Chapman. It was entirely put up by the oldest of the Italians in Providence.

Then there are the corroborating stories of Weeks, Madeiros' associate now a lifer in the Charlestown Penitentiary, of the owners of the Blue Bird Inn, of various Providence lawyers and policemen as to the activities of the Morelli gang.

Out of this comparatively understandable world of thieves and murderers, the affidavits lead us into the underground passages of the Department of Justice, into a world of dicks and stoolpigeons.

Here are the three main affidavits. They speak for themselves.

AFFIDAVIT OF LAWRENCE LETHERMAN

My name is Lawrence Letherman. I live in Malden, and am in the employ of the Beacon Trust Company. I was in the Federal service for thirty-six years, first in the railway mail service for nine years; then as Post Office Inspector for twenty five years; then three years as local agent of the Department of Justice in Boston in charge of the Bureau of Investigation. I began the last named duties in September, 1921.

While I was Post Office Inspector I co-operated to a considerable extent with the agents of the Department of Justice in Boston in matters of joint concern, including the Sacco-Vanzetti case. The man under me in direct charge of matters relating to that case was Mr. William West, who is still attached to the Department of Justice in Boston. I know that Mr. West co-operated with Mr, Katzmann, the District Attorney, during the trial of the case, and later with Mr. Williams. I know that before, during, and after the trial of Sacco and Vanzetti Mr. West had a number of so-called "under cover" men assigned to this case, including one Ruzzamenti and one Carbone. I know that by an arrangement with the Department of Justice, Carbone was placed in a cell next to the cell of Sacco for the purpose of obtaining whatever incriminating information he could obtain from Sacco, after winning his confidence. Nothing, however, was obtained in that way. One Weiss, formerly an agent of the Department, was involved in this plan. He was running a private office at that time on the seventh floor of the building at 7 Water Street under the offices of the Department, and remained in touch with the Department agents. Efforts were made by Mr. West to put other men in the Dedham Jail as spies, but the men whom he desired to use for that purpose objected.

Before, during, and after the trial, the Department of Justice had a number of men assigned to watch the activities of the Sacco-Vanzetti Defense Committee. No evidence warranting prosecution of anybody was obtained by these men. They were all "under cover" men, and one or two of them obtained employment by the Committee in some capacity or other. I think one of them was a collector. The Department of Justice in Boston was anxious to get sufficient evidence against Sacco and Vanzetti to deport them, but never succeeded in getting the kind and amount of evidence required for that purpose. It was the opinion of the Department agents here that a conviction of Sacco and Vanzetti for murder would be one way of disposing of these two men. It was also the general opinion of such agents in Boston as had any actual knowledge of the Sacco-Vanzetti case; that Sacco and Vanzetti, although anarchists and agitators, were not highway robbers, and had nothing to do with the South Braintree crime. My opinion, and the opinion of most of the older men in the Government service, has always been that the South Braintree crime was the work of professionals.

The Boston agents of the Department of Justice assigned certain men to attend the trial of Sacco and Vanzetti, including Mr. Weyand. Mr. West also attended the trial. There is or was a great deal of correspondence on file in the Boston office between Mr. West and Mr. Katzmann, the District Attorney, and there are also copies of reports sent to Washington about the case. Letters and reports were made in triplicate; two copies were sent to Washington and one retained in Boston. The letters and documents on file in the Boston office would throw a great deal of light upon the preparation of the Sacco-Vanzetti case for trial, and upon the real opinion of the Boston office of the Department of Justice as to the guilt of Sacco and Vanzetti of the particular crime with which they were charged.

I know that at one time Mr. West placed an Italian printer or linotyper in the office of some Italian newspaper in Boston for the purpose of obtaining information. One of the men employed by West at one stage of the Sacco-Vanzetti case was named Shaughnessy. He was subsequently convicted of highway robbery and is now serving a term in the Massachusetts State Prison. One of the "under cover" men employed by Mr. West was an Armenian named Harold Zorian. While being paid $7.00 a day by the Government he became Secretary of some Communist or Radical organization in the vicinity of Boston, the proceedings of which he reported to the Department.

(So the government *was* interested in the conviction of Sacco and Vanzetti? Provocative agents *were* used to gain the confidence of the Defense Committee? The Department of Justice *is* in possession of evidence and information about the case?

"Have Attorney General Sargent and his subordinates..... stooped so low and are they so degraded that they are willing by the concealment of evidence to enter into a fraudulent conspiracy with the government of Massachusetts to send two men to the electric chair, not because they were murderers but because they were radicals?" asks Judge Thayer in his decision).

AFFIDAVIT OF FRED J. WEYAND

My name is Fred J. Weyand. I reside in Portland, Maine. I am a Special Agent of the Attorney General's office of the State of Maine, and have been since I resigned as an agent of the Department of Justice about a year and a half ago.

I became connected with the Department of Justice in the year 1916, and shortly afterwards became a Special Agent with an office first at 24 Milk Street, Boston, later at 45 Milk Street and later at 7 Water Street, where the Department had offices on the eighth floor, and later at the Post Office Building. My duties as Special Agent were in general to investigate and report upon any and all violations of the penal code which I might be assigned to investigate by my superiors, who were first Frederick Smith, next George E. Kelliher, next John Hannahan, next

Charles Bancroft and last Lawrence Letherman. These were my superiors while I was working from the Boston office. I occasionally worked in other parts of the country and then came under other superiors temporarily. I was a Special Agent during the entire administration of Mitchell Palmer, Attorney General of the United States, and was concerned in the activities against the so-called Reds or Radicals, including arrests and deportations which were instigated by Mr. Palmer, and which included the wholesale raids made in the month of January 1920, in some of which I participated.

Sometime before the arrest of Sacco and Vanzetti on May 5, 1920—just how long before I do not remember—the names of both of them had got in the files of the Department of Justice as Radicals to be watched. The Boston files of the Department, including correspondence, would show the date when the names of these men were first brought to the attention of the Department. Both these men were listed as followers or associates of an educated Italian editor named Galleani. Galleani was the publisher of an anarchistic paper. He lived in Wrentham and published his paper, I think, in Lynn. Among other persons associated with Galleani were Carlo Tresca, Carlo Valdinoci and David Tedesco. The suspicion entertained by the Department of Justice against Sacco and Vanzetti was that they had violated the Selective Service Act, and also that they were anarchists or held Radical opinions of some sort or other.

A man named Feri Felix Weiss was transferred from the Immigration Bureau to the Department of Justice in Boston in the year 1917, and remained a Special Agent of that Department in Boston until 1919,I think. He then travelled abroad and returned in 1920 and opened an office as a scientific detective and lecturer at 7 Water Street, Boston, with an office on the floor below occupied by the Department of Justice. In 1925, Weiss returned to the Immigration Department at Boston, where he is at the present time.

William J. West, who is now a Special Agent of the Department of Justice, became such in July or August 1917. Prior to that he was an Immigration Inspector with Feri Weiss. Since his appointment as a Special Agent he has spent most of his time in the Boston office of the Department of Justice, having in charge during the past seven years the so-called Radical Division of the Department of Justice, which has been in operation since about 1917.

During the year 1920 I did a good deal of work in the State of Maine, but was in Boston for several days at least once every two weeks. I have knowledge that the result of the trial before

Judge Anderson of the Radicals or Communists, as we called them, arrested at the time of the raids above referred to, and of the decision of Judge Anderson freeing many of them and of his criticisms of the Department of Justice, was to make all agents of the Department of Justice in Boston more cautious afterwards in proceeding against suspected Radicals.

Shortly after the arrest of Sacco and Vanzetti on the charge of the South Braintree murders, meetings began to be held by sympathizers, and I was assigned to attend these meetings and report to the Department the speeches made. We also assigned a certain "under cover" man, as we called him, to win the confidence of the Sacco-Vanzetti Defense Committee, and to become one of the collectors. This man used to report the proceedings of the Committee to the Department agents in Boston, and has said to me he was in the habit of taking as much money collected for his own use as he saw fit. So far as I know, no evidence was obtained of utterances at any of these meetings which warranted proceedings against anybody. Mr. West was also attending meetings of Sacco-Vanzetti sympathizers during the same period. The original reports thus obtained were sent to the Washington office of the Department of Justice and duplicates kept in the Boston office, where I believe they now are. I know that at one time as many as twelve agents of the Department of Justice located in Boston were assigned to cover Sacco-Vanzetti meetings and other Radical activities connected with the Sacco-Vanzetti case. No evidence was discovered warranting the institution of proceedings against anybody. I have no present recollection of the trial of Vanzetti for the alleged Bridgewater robbery; but when the joint trial of Sacco and Vanzetti for the South Braintree murders began in the summer of 1921, the Department of Justice at Boston took an active interest in the matter. I was assigned to cover the trial for the purpose of reporting the proceedings and picking up any information that I could in regard to the Radical activities of Sacco and Vanzetti, or of any of their friends. Mr. West also attended the trial for the same purpose. I was not personally in touch with Mr. Katzmann, the District Attorney, or his office, but Mr. West was in touch with them and was giving and obtaining information in regard to the case.

Going back now before the trial, a certain John Ruzzamenti had been informally employed by special agents of the Department of Justice from some time in the year 1917, to furnish information concerning Radical activities and evasion of the draft by Italians, and in this connection had made an investigation of Tedesco, above referred to, who was once arrested in consequence

of information furnished by Ruzzamenti, but was never tried.
During this time Ruzzamenti also worked occasionally for
detective agencies. He was well known to Weiss.

I have been informed by Mr. West and believe, and therefore
allege, that there was another Italian whom the Department
occasionally used for similar purposes, named Carbone and that
he, under an arrangement with the District Attorney, the Sheriff,
and Mr. Weiss, was placed in the cell next to the cell of Sacco
sometime during the year 1920 for the purpose of winning the
confidence of Sacco, and thus of obtaining, if he could, incriminating evidence against him, but no evidence of the sort was
obtained by Carbone. The primary purpose of the Department
in putting Carbone there was to obtain evidence, if possible,
concerning the so-called Wall Street explosion; but it was also
hoped that other incriminating evidence might be obtained.

Sometime in the early part of the year 1921, I was informed
by Ruzzamenti that he had been sent for by Weiss, who was
then out of Government service, to come on here to help convict
Sacco and Vanzetti; that he had seen Katzmann, and that an
arrangement had been made by which he was to secure board
in the house of Mrs. Sacco and obtain her confidence, and thus
obtain information; but that arrangement had never been
carried out, and he had not been paid. I annex to this affidavit
photostatic copies of parts of a letter which I identify as in the
handwriting of Weiss.

Shortly after the trial of Sacco and Vanzetti was concluded
I said to Weiss that I did not believe they were the right men,
meaning the men who shot the paymaster, and he replied that
that might be so, but that they were bad actors and would get
what they deserved anyway.

Instructions were received from the Chief of the Bureau of
the Department of Justice in Washington from time to time in
reference to the Sacco-Vanzetti case. They are on file or should
be on file in the Boston office.

The understanding in this case between the agents of the
Department of Justice in Boston and the District Attorney
followed the usual custom, that the Department of Justice would
help the District Attorney to secure a conviction, and that he in
turn would help the agents of the Department of Justice to
secure information that they might desire. This would include
the turning over of any pertinent information by the Department
of Justice to the District Attorney. Sacco and Vanzetti were,
at least in the opinion of the Boston agents of the Department of
Justice, not liable to deportation as draft dodgers, but only as
anarchists, and could not be deported as anarchists unless it

could be shown that they were believers in anarchy, which is always a difficult thing to show. It usually can only be shown by self-incrimination. The Boston agents believed that these men were anarchists, and hoped to be able to secure the necessary evidence against them from their testimony at their trial for murder, to be used in case they were not convicted for murder. There is correspondence between Mr. Katzmann and Mr. West on file in the Boston office of the Department. Mr. West furnished Mr. Katzmann information about the Radical activities of Sacco and Vanzetti to be used in their cross-examination.

In the years 1922-1924 Mr. West had working for him as "under cover" or secret operators an Italian and a Syrian or Armenian. The Italian worked as a printer. I do not remember the names of either of them; but I know that he put the Italian in as a linotyper in the office of an Italian newspaper in Boston as a spy. The Syrian or Armenian is the man to whom I have referred above as having become a collector for the Committee.

From my investigation, combined with the investigation made by the other agents of the Department in Boston, I am convinced not only that these men had violated the Selective Service rules and regulations and evaded the draft, but that they were anarchists, and that they ought to have been deported. By calling these men anarchists, I do not mean necessarily that they were inclined to violence, nor do I understand all the different meanings that different people would attach to the word "anarchists". What I mean is that I think they did not believe in organized government or in private property. But I am also thoroughly convinced and always have been, and I believe that is and always has been the opinion of such Boston agents of the Department of Justice as had any knowledge on the subject, that these men had nothing whatever to do with the South Braintree murders, and that their conviction was the result of co-operation between the Boston agents of the Department of Justice and the District Attorney. It was the general opinion of the Boston agents of the Department of Justice having knowledge of the affair that the South Braintree crime was committed by a gang of professional highwaymen.

I annex hereto a picture of Mr. Feri Felix Weiss printed on the outside of one of his advertisements.

So ends as fine a picture of the inner workings of the Spanish Inquisition as has seen the light in many a day. I can't help quoting again Judge Thayer's very pertinent question:

"Have Attorney General Sargent and his subordinates... stooped so low and are they so degraded that they are willing by the concealment of evidence to enter into a fraudulent conspiracy with the government of Massachusetts to send two men to the electric chair, not because they were murderers but because they were radicals?"

AFFIDAVIT OF JOHN RUZZAMENTI

John Ruzzamenti being first duly sworn, on oath deposes and says that he is now and has been for upwards of thirty days last past a resident of the City of Boston, County of Suffolk and Commonwealth of Massachusetts.

That in the month of December 1920 the affiant resided in the town of Reddington, State of Pennsylvania, and was employed in the capacity of brass melter in the Reddington Standard Fitting Corporation, a subsidiary of the Bethlehem Steel Corporation.

That sometime in December 1920 and to the affiant's best knowledge, information and belief, about December 18th or 19th, he, the affiant, received through the United States Post Office an envelope bearing Boston post-mark and stamped with special delivery stamp and containing the name and address of affiant. That inside of said envelope was another sealed envelope bearing on the outside the notation "burn this after you have read". That inside of said sealed envelope was a letter purporting to come from one Feri Felix Weiss. That affiant well knew said Weiss having worked with and been employed by said Weiss when said Weiss was employed by the United States Department of Justice at Boston specially assigned to so-called Red or Radical cases. That the affiant then had in his possession a card of said Weiss reading as follows, to-wit:

AMERICAN AND FOREIGN CONNECTIONS

Cable Address Feriweiss   P. O. Box 2107 Boston

FERI   FELIX   WEISS

Scientific-Secret-Service
Licensed and Bonded — Modern Scientific Methods

FORMERLY WITH

Bureau of Investigation, U. S. Department of Justice
Immigration Service, U. S. Department of Labor
Translation Section; Military Intelligence
Branch U. S. War Department.

That the said letter contained in said envelope read as follows, to-wit:

December 17, 1920

My dear John:

Just returned from a trip I found your two letters, and answer them by return mail.

Would you like to help me on a case which I may clinch here? It is the case of Sacco and Vanzetti, who are in jail awaiting trial for having shot the paymaster of the South Braintree shoe-factory.

Do you know these fellows? They are members of the Galleani gang, and Sacco used to work in the Cordage works in Plymouth.

He also worked in the Plant shoe factory.

It is a very important case, and I need a clever Italian who would mix with the gang, and if necessary even stay in jail for a few days just to find out what they say.

How much pay would you want?

You would have to come right away.

Do you think you could work amongst them?

I am not sure whether they might know you from Milford, though I don't think that Sacco was ever there.

If we are successful in this venture, we might tackle the big Wall Street affair in New York, as all the other agencies are up against a wall in that matter.

Let me know by the return envelope which I herewith enclose.

I must give my friends an answer not later than Monday, so you must mail your answer to me immediately. Don't write me a long letter, just say "yes, I'll work for $8" a day, or whatever you want, so I can put it up to my friend.

In case you get my letter only Sunday, better telegraph me your answer, P. O. Box 2107. Just say "Yes, $8" "John".

I am afraid they won't pay $8, so make it less if you can.

Of course any expenses would be extra.

If we deliver the goods they will probably give us the reward.

I think there is $2,000 written out.

You would have to start as soon as possible, probably after Christmas, if you care to stay with your folks over the holidays.

Best regards to Mrs. R. and the children.

With best of wishes, believe me,

Your friend

F—i

That immediately upon receipt of said letter the affiant well knowing from past experience with said Weiss the need of expedition and secrecy, instructed his wife, Laura Ruzzamenti, to telegraph to said Feri Felix Weiss, P. O. Box 2107, Boston Mass. in substance and effect that he, the affiant would come to Boston immediately after the Christmas holidays, and said telegram as outlined above was sent.

That between the said date of sending of said telegram to said Feri Felix Weiss and the morning of December 27th, 1920 when the affiant secured leave of absence from said Reddington Standard Fitting Corporation, and left Reddington, Pennsylvania to come to the City of Boston, no letter or telegram or communication of any character was received by the affiant from the said Feri Felix Weiss.

That upon arrival in the City of Boston, Commonwealth of Massachusetts, on the evening of December 27th, 1920, at or about the hour of ten p. m., the affiant went to the office of said Feri Felix Weiss at 7 Water Street in the City of Boston and made inquiry for said Weiss, but found that he was out for the evening. Whereupon the affiant went to the American House in said City of Boston and there registered.

That following morning, December 28th, 1920, the affiant went to the office of said Feri Felix Weiss at 7 Water Stret in said City of Boston and interviewed the said Weiss.

That the said Weiss then admitted receipt of affiant's telegram but expressed some surprise that the affiant had come to the City of Boston in view of the fact that the said Weiss had sent to him, the affiant, a telegram stating that he should not come.

That the affiant has since made inquiry and to the best of his knowledge, information and belief the said Weiss did not send a telegram to the affiant, but did send a letter stating in effect that he, the affiant, was not to come to Boston until further word was received from the said Weiss, but that said letter was not received in Reddington, Pennsylvania, until December 28th, 1920, the day after the affiant left Reddington, Pennsylvania.

That after some discussion the said Weiss stated to the affiant in substance and effect that however it was all right: that he, the affiant, was here in Boston and that he, the said Weiss, would immediately get in touch with Mr. Frederick G. Katzmann, the District Attorney for Norfolk and Plymouth Counties, Commonwealth of Massachusetts, and would arrange for an interview between the said Katzmann and the affiant.

That the said Weiss in the presence of affiant attempted to telephone the said Frederick G. Katzmann, but was unable at that time to secure a connection at the office of said Katzmann at Hyde Park, Commonwealth of Massachusetts.

That thereafter, to-wit, December 28th and December 29th 1920, the affiant remained in and about the office of said Weiss discussing with said Weiss and receiving from said Weiss the details of the plan purporting to be the product of the minds of said Weiss and said Katzmann and mutually agreed upon between said Weiss and said Katzmann, the details of which plan are hereinafter set forth, and also awaiting instructions from said Weiss as to when he, the affiant, should see the said Katzmann; that sometime in the afternoon of December 29th, 1920 the affiant received instructions from said Weiss to be at the office of said Katzmann at said Hyde Park the morning of December 30th, 1920 at nine a. m.

That in accordance with said instructions the affiant at nine a. m. on December 30th, 1920 was at the office of said Frederick G. Katzmann, District Attorney of Norfolk and Plymouth Counties, Commonwealth of Massachusetts, at Hyde Park, Massachusetts, and there awaited the coming of said Katzmann, that shortly after nine a. m. the affiant saw a gentleman enter the said building and go upstairs; that thereupon the affiant followed the said party and saw him turn to the door marked with the name of said Katzmann and insert a key; that the affiant then stepped up to said party, whereupon the said party turned and said to him, the affiant, "Is that you John?" whereupon the affiant admitted his identity and was welcomed into the office by said Katzmann, the said Katzmann helping the affiant to remove his overcoat; that the affiant then explained to said Katzmann that he had been sent there by said Weiss and presented as evidence of his identity the card of said Weiss with the name of the affiant written in the handwriting of said Weiss on the back of said card.

That immediately after the identity of the affiant was established to the satisfaction of said Katzmann, the said Katzmann asked the affiant in substance and effect what he had to say of importance; whereupon the affiant outlined to the said

Katzmann the proposition or plan that had been proposed to the affiant by said Weiss, and which the affiant had been told was the product of the minds of Weiss and said Katzmann, which was in substance and effect that he, the affiant, was by prearranged plan and in concert with police officers to break and enter some dwelling house for the ostensible purpose of committing the crime of burglary, and that by prearranged plan with said police officers the affiant was to be apparently caught in the act of committing the crime of burglary; that then the affiant would be duly and regularly arrested, complaint issued, committment papers executed and the affiant confined under the terms of said committment in the Dedham County Jail in Norfolk County, Commonwealth of Massachusetts, the said jail being the jail where Nicola Sacco, named in the title herein, was then confined and awaiting trial on the charge of murder.

That then by prearranged plan and in concert and with the understanding of one Samuel Capen, High Sheriff of Norfolk County, Commonwealth of Massachusetts, the affiant would be placed in a cell next to and adjoining to the one occupied by said Sacco, and that the affiant would then, by preconceived plan and by special arrangement with said High Sheriff of Norfolk County, be given special privileges and special opportunity to establish the confidence of and to act as a stool pigeon on said Nicola Sacco. That in this connection the said Weiss had instructed the affiant that he, the affiant, was upon his incarceration to appear to be very much depressed and melancholy by reason of his arrest and was to make no attempt to talk with said Sacco for at least three days after his arrest. That the affiant outlining the said plan to the said Katzmann as same had been outlined to the affiant by said Weiss, stated to the said Katzmann that he, the affiant, had never been arrested and was not agreeable to this plan of arrest; that while he, the affiant, had been previously engaged by the said Weiss as an operative while the said Weiss was in the United States Department of Justice, nevertheless the affiant had never up to that time ever gone so far as to commit a crime in the furtherance of any end, and that he, the affiant, could not and would not agree to the said plan of said Weiss, but was willing to listen to any counter suggestion or other proposition that might be made by the said Katzmann.

That thereupon the said Katzmann said to the affiant in substance and effect that he, the said Katzmann, was right hard up against it; that he, the said Katzmann, had no evidence as against the said Nicola Sacco or as against the said Bartolomeo Vanzetti, that they, the said Sacco and said Vanzetti, had not

talked and would not talk; that he had been unable to get anything out of them or out of any other person, that said
Katzmann named in this connection some man that he had
arrested in connection with a motorcycle, and stated that
he had grilled this man but had been unable to learn anything,
and that it was necessary that he secure other and additional
testimony to that which he already had. Whereupon with this
preliminary explanation, the said Katzmann made the following
proposition, to wit:

That Rosina Sacco or Rose Sacco, the wife of said Nicola
Sacco, resided in the town of Stoughton, Commonwealth of
Massachusetts and there had a small home and had an extra and
unused room in said house by reason of the arrest and incarceration of her husband, and he, the said Katzmann, then
proposed to the affiant that he, the affiant, should undertake to
secure employment in said town of Stoughton or some place
adjacent thereto and should as an Italian and a member of the
same race as the said Rosina or Rose Sacco, secure a room in her
home, and that for and by reason of the fact that the said Rosina
or Rose Sacco was undergoing great physical, mental and
spiritual suffering by reason of the incarceration of her husband,
it should be easy for the affiant to establish friendly relations
with her, and said relations once established, it would then be
easy for the affiant to secure confidential communications from
her as to any criminal activities of her husband, the said Nicola
Sacco. That the affiant agreed to undertake this plan.

That thereupon the said Katzmann stated to the affiant that
it would be some few days before he, the said Katzmann, was
ready to go ahead, that meanwhile he, the affiant, was to "send
me" (Katzmann) "your expense bill and I will see that it goes
through the County and you will get your money." That the
affiant then left the said Katzmann's office, the said Katzmann
courteously helping the affiant to put on his overcoat and following him to the door and shaking hands in parting.

That the affiant then returned to Boston and reported to
said Feri Felix Weiss. That the day following affiant sent his
statement to said Katzmann. That meanwhile it was arranged
between the affiant and said Weiss that he, the affiant, would be
employed by said Weiss pending word from said Katzmann on
a job down on Cape Cod; that thereupon he, the affiant, went to
Cape Cod on said investigation for said Weiss and was employed
for a period of approximately two weeks; that nothing developing
and the affiant receiving no word from said Weiss, he, the
affiant, returned to Pennsylvania sometime about the middle of
January 1921.

That after the affiant returned to Pennsylvania he received a letter from said Weiss, only a part of said letter being now in the possession of the affiant; the part which he now has reading on the face thereof as follows, to wit:

"Dear John:
I just returned from my trip and found your letters. As soon as Mr. Katzmann sends me your check I'll mail it to you."

and on the back thereof as follows, to-wit:

"was a big trial of Mrs. De Falco.   I'll remind him by and by of your bill.
I am sorry I could not see you before you went home.
With kindest regards to you and your family, believe me
Your friend,
FERI"

That after a number of letters written by the affiant to the said Weiss and to the said Katzmann, the affiant received another letter from said Weiss reading as follows, to-wit:

"My dear John:
I got your letters about collecting money from District Attorney Katzmann.
As much as I regret that you have such a hard time with your children being out of work, I am not blind to facts, and feel I must enlighten you.
First of all you must remember that you came here of your own will.   Nobody told you to come to Boston. I telegraphed clearly that you should only come when I write you.   You did not wait for my letter.   I then did the next best thing for you, and employed you on the Cape.
Then Katzmann said he might pay you.   So put in your bill, as promised, but have not heard from him. It will be a good thing if you write to him personally about it; he probably will hurry it along.
But remember, that you can force neither him nor me to pay your expenses, as there was absolutely no agreement to that effect between him, me and you. Keep this clearly in your mind.
It is foolish to send your wife here, as that only makes additional expense, without any result.   A letter to Katzmann will do just as well.

If I was fixed better financially, I would gladly send you the money, as I regarded you always as my friend, and am always sorry for anybody with a large family to support at the present time.   But I have a hard pull myself.

That is all I can say today.   Hoping to hear from Katzmann soon, or that you hear from him if you write, believe me,

Sincerely yours,

FERI.

Let me know if he sends you a check, so that I should not bother him afterwards thinking that you did not get it."

That the wife of the affiant, Laura Ruzzamenti, sometime in the spring of 1921, to-wit in the month of April, called on the said Katzmann and presented the claim of her husband and asked that same be paid.

That said claim for transportation, time and expenses has not been paid by said Katzmann or said Weiss or by any person notwithstanding the fact that the affiant has made many and divers efforts to secure said pay, same consisting of the sending of the statement of transportation, time and expenses in accordance with request of said Katzmann on the day following the interview of December 30th, 1920; and the sending of a great number of letters written by the affiant to the said Katzmann.   That said statement has not been paid and said letters have not been answered.

Signed JOHN RUZZAMENTI

(In this connection we must insert the letter of Feri Felix Weiss that did not come into Mr. Thompson's hands until several weeks after the hearing.   Here are his affidavit and Weiss's letter that completes the picture.)

AFFIDAVIT OF WILLIAM G. THOMPSON

My name is William G. Thompson.   I am counsel for the defendants in the above entitled case.   On or about Sept. 21 last I learned from Mr. Frank P. Sibley, a reporter on the *Boston Globe*, that that newspaper had just received a letter from Feri Felix Weiss, with a request that it be published, but that the

Globe did not intend to publish the letter. Shortly afterward I began efforts to obtain this letter, and succeeded in doing so to-day, Oct. 7, with it was the envelope in which it was received at the Globe office. I annex said original letter and said envelope hereto, and make them part of this affidavit.

As I remember it, there is a fac-simile of the signature of Weiss on the picture of him annexed to the affidavit of Fred J. Weyand. I also call attention to the fact that this letter is written upon a letterhead stamped with the name of said Weiss, and was received in an envelope also stamped with his name in the upper left hand corner.

In connection with this letter I call attention to the contents of the letter of said Weiss to John Ruzzamenti on file in the case, a fac-simile of a part of which is also annexed to the affidavit of said Weyand, and of the following statements therein—namely, letter dated Dec. 17, 1920:

> "Would you like to help me on a case which I may clinch here? It is the case of Sacco and Vanzetti, who are in jail awaiting trial for having shot the paymaster of the South Braintree shoe factory. * * * It is a very important case, and I need a clever Italian who would mix with the gang, and, if necessary, even stay in jail for a few days just to find out what they say. * * * I am afraid they won't pay $8, so make it less if you can. Of course any expenses would be extra. If we deliver the goods they will probably give us the reward. I think there is $2,000 written out."

In connection with this letter I also call attention to the parts of the affidavits of Weyand and Letherman relating to the activities and purposes of said Weiss in connection with the prosecution of Sacco and Vanzetti. I also, in connection with this letter, call attention to the affidavit of Mr. Katzmann on file in this case. I especially desire to call attention to the following sentences in this letter, namely:

> "I explained to him (Katzmann) that anarchists do not commit crimes for money, but for a principle, and that banditry was not in their code", and
> "The truth in the "framing" was that we intended to put Ruzzamenti in with Sacco as much to clear Sacco of any guilt in the Braintree affair as to find him guilty."

Signed WILLIAM G. THOMPSON

LETTER OF FERI FELIX WEISS

The letter annexed to the affidavit follows:

Chicago, Ill., Sept. 19, 1926

Editor, *Boston Globe*,
Boston, Mass.

Dear Sir:—

It has just come to my attention—stationed as I am in the Government service in the West—that my name has been mentioned in your account of the "Sacco and Vanzetti" affair through an affidavit by former District Attorney Katzmann on one hand, and the connection of Ruzzamenti on the other.

The facts, as far as I am concerned with this case, are as follows:

Katzmann sent for me at the time to learn what I knew about Sacco, having been Special Agent of the United States Department of Justice in charge of investigations covering anarchists and similar criminals whose aim was the forceful overthrow of the Government of the United States. I told Katzmann that I knew that Sacco was an active anarchist, connected with the famous or notorious Galleani group of Lynn, Mass., who had bomb-outrages on the brain. When Katzmann asked me what I thought of Sacco as a participant in the Braintree hold-up, I explained to him that anarchists do not commit crimes for money but for a principle, and that banditry was not in their code.

It was at the suggestion of Katzmann that I wrote the undercover informant Ruzzamenti whether he was willing to go to jail and share the cell with Sacco to find out what Sacco had to tell about his connection with the Braintree affair. Ruzzamenti did not answer this letter by a letter, but took the first train from Pennsylvania to Boston. Though this was against my arrangement with him, I faced the situation, and sent him to Katzmann, who had agreed over the phone to talk to Ruzzamenti regarding the plan we had in mind. Katzmann then decided, after a talk with Ruzzamenti, that he better drop the matter.

Ruzzamenti tried to collect expenses from Katzmann, but failed. Then Ruzzamenti turned around and sold out to the defense. He used my letter to him as evidence. The first I knew of Ruzzamenti's treachery was when I received a warning from a friendly source in Spain to the effect that my letter had been broadcasted in mimeograph form to aid in the collection of funds for the Sacco and Vanzetti defense. My friend sent me warning lest the rabid Latin anarchists should take it into their heads to "get square" with me for trying to "frame Sacco."

The truth in the "framing" was that we intended to put
Ruzzamenti in with Sacco as much to clear Sacco of any guilt
in the Braintree affair as to find him guilty! I had no interest
whatsoever in railroading an innocent man to the electric chair,
and Lawyer Thompson's reference to me as "being heartless" is
absurd, if not ridiculous. My entire connection with this case
was outlined here, and my only motive in trying to clear up the
mystery was to aid justice.

That I should be abused and besmirched with mud by both
sides, the defense as well as the District Attorney, when I acted
as any patriotic citizen would to protect the life and property of
all, is a sad reflection upon legal ethics in Massachusetts. I
leave it to the public to pass judgment in view of the above
cited facts. That Katzmann is trying to wash his hands of the
Ruzzamenti fiasco, putting the blame on me; that Ruzzamenti
delivered my life into the hands of the international Reds the
world over by his treachery, reminds me of the two characters in
the New Testament who always seem to enjoy a resurrection:
Pontius Pilate and Judas Iscariot.

Respectfully,

FERI FELIX WEISS

*"Have Attorney General Sargent and his subordinates...
stooped so low, and are they so degraded that they are willing
by the concealment of evidence to enter into a fraudulent
conspiracy with the government of Massachusetts to send two
men to the electric chair, not because they were murderers but
because they were radicals?"*

(All attempts on the part of the defense to secure information
from the Department of Justice files on the case have so far
proved fruitless. Chief Counsel Thompson has written the
Attorney General of the United States on the subject and in
spite of the intercession of Senator Butler of Massachusetts,
received no satisfactory reply. The Department of Justice
refuses to give up its secrets.)

Where are Sacco and Vanzetti in all this? A broken man
in Charlestown, a broken man in a grey birdcage in Dedham,
struggling to keep some shreds of human dignity in face of the
Chair? Not at all.

Circumstances sometimes force men into situations so dramatic, thrust their puny frames so far into the burning bright searchlights of history that they or their shadows on men's minds become enormous symbols. Sacco and Vanzetti are all the immigrants who have built this nation's industries with their sweat and their blood and have gotten for it nothing but the smallest wage it was possible to give them and a helot's position under the bootheels of the Arrow Collar social order. They are all the wops, hunkies, bohunks, factory fodder that hunger drives into the American mills through the painful sieve of Ellis Island. They are the dreams of a saner social order of those who can't stand the law of dawg eat dawg. This tiny courtroom is a focus of the turmoil of an age of tradition, the center of eyes all over the world. Sacco and Vanzetti throw enormous shadows on the courthouse walls.

William G. Thompson feels all this dimly when, the last affidavit read, he pauses to begin his argument. But mostly he feels that as a citizen it is his duty to protect the laws and liberties of his state and as a man to try to save two innocent men from being murdered by a machine set going in a moment of hatred and panic. He is a broadshouldered man with steely white hair and a broad forehead and broad cheekbones. He doesn't mince words. He feels things intensely. The case is no legal game of chess for him.

"I rest my case on these affidavits, on the other five propositions that I have argued, but if they all fail, and I cannot see how they can, I rest my case on that rock alone, on the sixth proposition in my brief—innocent or guilty, right or wrong, foolish or wise men—these men ought not now to be sentenced to death for this crime so long as they have the right to say, "The government of this great country put spies in my cell, planned to put spies in my wife's house, they put spies on my friends, took money that they were collecting to defend me, put it in their own pocket and joked about it and said they don't believe I am guilty but will help convict me, because they could not get enough evidence to deport me under the laws of Congress, and were willing as one of them continually said to adopt the method of killing me for murder as one way to get rid of me."

Ranney's handling of the case has been pretty perfunctory throughout, he has contented himself with trying to destroy the Court's opinion of Madeiros' veracity. A criminal is only to be believed when he speaks to his own detriment.   He presents affidavits of the Morelli's and their friends denying that they had ever heard of Madeiros, tries to imply that Letherman and Weyand were fired from the government employ and had no right to betray the secrets of their department.   He knows that he does not need to make much effort.   He is strong in the inertia of the courts.   The defence will have to exert six times the energy of the prosecution to overturn the dead weighty block of six other motions denied.

Thompson comes back at him with a phrase worthy of Patrick Henry.

...."And I will say to your honor that a government that has come to honor its own secrets more than the lives of its citizens has become a tyranny whether you call it a republic or monarchy or anything else."

Then the dry, crackling, careful voice of Judge Thayer and the hearing is adjourned.

Hear ye, hear ye, hear ye, all who have had business before the honorable the justice of the superior court of the south-eastern district of Massachusetts will now disperse.   The court is adjourned without day.

God Save the Commonwealth of Massachusetts.

The Court refused to grant a new trial.   The Court has decided that Sacco and Vanzetti must die.

God Save the Commonwealth of Massachusetts.

III

THE RED DELIRIUM

How is all this possible?   Why were these men ever convicted in the first place?   From the calm of the year of our Lord 1926 it's pretty hard to remember the delirious year 1920.

On June 3rd 1919 a bomb exploded outside the Washington house of Attorney General A. Mitchell Palmer. In the previous months various people had received bombs through the mail, one of them blowing off the two hands of the unfortunate housemaid who undid the package. No one, and least of all the federal detectives ever seems to have discovered who committed these outrages or why they were committed. But their result was to put a scare into every public official in the country, and particularly into Attorney General Palmer. No one knew where the lightning would strike next. The signing of peace had left the carefully stirred up hatred of the war years unsatisfied. It was easy for people who knew what they were doing to turn the terrors of government officials and the unanalyzed feeling of distrust of foreigners of the average man into a great crusade of hate against reds, radicals, dissenters of all sorts. The Department of Justice, backed by the press, frenziedly acclaimed by the man on the street, invented an immanent revolution. All the horrors of Russian Bolshevism were about to be enacted on our peaceful shores. That fall the roundup began. Every man had his ear to his neighbor's keyhole. This first crusade culminated in the sailing of the Buford, the "soviet ark" loaded with alien "anarchists" and in the preparation of the famous list of eighty thousand radicals who were to be gotten out of the way.

But that was not enough to satisfy the desire for victims of the country at large, and the greed of the detectives and anti-labor operatives of different sorts who were making a fat living off the Department of Justice. So the January raids were planned.

The following paragraph from Louis F. Post's book shows that he, seeing the thing from the inside as Assistant Secretary of Labor, felt that the hysteria was being pretty consciously directed:

"The whole red crusade seems to have been saturated with 'labor spy' interests—the interests, that is, of private detective agencies which, in the secret service of masterful corporations, were engaged generating and in intensifying industrial suspicions and hatreds. It was under these influences, apparently, that the appropriations authorized by Congress "for the detection and prosecution of crimes" exclusively, were in part diverted to the rounding-up of aliens, not as criminals but as the possible subjects for administrative deportation."

The January raids were aimed at the "Communists."

"Hardly had the year nineteen-twenty opened" says the former Assistant Secretary of Labor, "when the Department of Justice entered upon the red crusade for which its raiding of the preceding November had been a tryout. Numerously recruited for the occasion from roughneck groups of the strikebreaking variety and actively supported by local police authorities, the detective auxiliary of the Department of Justice spent the night of the second day in January at raiding lawful assemblages in more than thirty cities and towns of the United States—thirty-three being the number officially reported. Their object was wholesale arrests in furtherance of the plans already outlined for mass deportations of alien members of the Communist and the Communist-Labor parties. The approximate number of arrests officially reported was 2,500."

The details can be read in the pamphlet on *Illegal Practices of the Department of Justice* prepared in May of the same year by a committee of twelve well-known lawyers.

Here is the preface to that pamphlet:

TO THE AMERICAN PEOPLE:

For more than six months we, the undersigned lawyers, whose sworn duty it is to uphold the Constitution and Laws of the United States, have seen with growing apprehension the continued violation of that Constitution and breaking of those Laws by the Department of Justice of the United States government.

Under the guise of a campaign for the suppression of radical activities, the office of the Attorney General, acting by its local agents throughout the country, and giving express instructions from Washington, has committed continual illegal acts. Wholesale arrests both of aliens and citizens have been made without warrant or any process of law; men and women have been jailed and held *incomunicado* without access of friends or counsel; homes have been entered without search-warrant and property seized and removed; other property has been wantonly destroyed; workingmen and workingwomen suspected of radical views have been shamefully abused and maltreated. Agents of the Department of Justice have been introduced into radical organizations for the purpose of informing upon their members or inciting them to activities; these agents have even been instructed from Washington to arrange meetings upon certain dates for the express object of facilitating wholesale raids and arrests. In support of these illegal acts, and to create sentiment in its favor, the Department of Justice has also constituted itself a propaganda bureau, and has sent to newspapers and magazines of this country quantities of material designed to excite public opinion against radicals, all at the expense of the government and outside the scope of the Attorney General's duties.

We make no argument in favor of any radical doctrine as such, whether Socialist, Communist or Anarchist. No one of us belongs to any of these schools of thought. Nor do we now raise any question as to the Constitutional protection of free speech and a free press. We are concerned solely with bringing to the attention of the American people the utterly illegal acts which have been committed by those charged with the highest duty of enforcing the laws—acts which have caused widespread suffering and unrest, have struck at the foundation of American free institutions, and have brought the name of our country into disrepute.

These acts may be grouped under the following heads:

(1) *Cruel and Unusual Punishments*:

The Eighth Amendment to the United States Constitution provides:

"Excessive bail shall not be required nor excessive
fines imposed, nor cruel and unusual punishments
inflicted."

Punishments of the utmost cruelty, and therefore unthinkable in America, have become usual. Great numbers of persons arrested, both aliens and citizens, have been threatened, beaten with blackjacks, or actually tortured * * *

(2) *Arrests without Warrant*:

The Fourth Amendment to the Constitution provides:

"The right of the people to be secure in their
persons, houses, papers, and effects, against unreasonable searches and seizures, shall not be violated, and no
warrants shall issue, but upon probable cause, supported
by oath or affirmation, and particularly describing the
place to be searched, and the persons or things to be
seized."

Many hundreds of citizens and aliens alike have been arrested in wholesale raids, without warrants or pretense of warrants. They have then either been released, or have been detained in police stations or jails for indefinite lengths of time while warrants were being applied for. This practice of making mass raids and mass arrests without warrant has resulted directly from the instructions, both written and oral, issued by the Department of Justice at Washington.

(3) *Unreasonable Searches and Seizures*:

The Fourth Amendment has been quoted above.

In countless cases agents of the Department of Justice have entered the homes, offices, or gathering places of persons suspected of radical affiliations, and, without pretense of any search warrant, have seized and removed property belonging to them for use by the Department of Justice. In many of these raids property which could not be removed or was not useful to the Department, was intentionally smashed and destroyed.

(4) *Provocative Agents*:

We do not question the right of the Department of Justice to use its agents in the Bureau of Investigation to ascertain when the law is being violated. But the American people have never tolerated the use of undercover provocative agents or "agents provocateurs," such as have been familiar in old Russia or Spain. Such agents have been introduced by the Department of Justice into the radical movements, have reached positions of influence therein, have occupied themselves with informing upon or instigating acts which might be declared criminal, and at the express direction of Washington have brought about meetings of radicals in order to make possible wholesale arrests at such meetings.

(5) *Compelling Persons to be Witnesses against Themselves*:

The Fifth Amendment provides as follows:

"No person * * * shall be compelled in any criminal case to be a witness against himself, nor be deprived of life, liberty, or property, without due process of law."

It has been the practice of the Department of Justice and its agents, after making illegal arrests without warrant, to question and to force admission from him by terrorism, which admissions were subsequently to be used against him in deportation proceedings.

(6) *Propaganda by the Department of Justice*:

The legal functions of the Attorney General are: to advise the Government on questions of law, and to prosecute persons who have violated federal statutes. For the Attorney General to go into the field of propaganda against radicals is a deliberate misuse of his office and a deliberate squandering of funds entrusted to him by Congress. * * *

Since these illegal acts have been committed by the highest legal powers in the United States, there is no final appeal from them except to the conscience and condemnation of the American people. American institutions have not in fact been protected by the Attorney General's ruthless suppression. On the contrary those institutions have been seriously undermined, and revolutionary unrest has been vastly intensified. No organizations of radicals acting through propaganda over the last six months could have created as much revolutionary sentiment in America as has been created by the acts of the Department of Justice itself.

Even were one to admit that there existed any serious "Red menace" before the Attorney General started his "unflinching war" against it, his campaign has been singularly fruitless. Out of the many thousands suspected by the Attorney General (he had already listed 60,000 by name and history on November 14, 1919, aliens and citizens) what do the figures show of net results? Prior to January 1, 1920, there were actually deported 263 persons. Since January 1 there have been actually deported 18 persons. Since January 1 there have been ordered deported an additional 529 persons, and warrants for 1,547 have been cancelled (after full hearings and consideration of the evidence) by Assistant Secretary of Labor Louis F. Post, to whose courageous re-establishment of American Constitutional Law in deportation proceedings are due the attacks that have been made upon him. The Attorney General has consequently got rid of 810 alien suspects, which, on his own showing, leaves him at least 59,160 persons (aliens and citizens) still to cope with.

It has always been the proud boast of America that this is a government of laws and not of men. Our Constitution and laws have been based on the simple elements of human nature. Free men cannot be driven and repressed; they must be led. Free men respect justice and follow truth, but arbitrary power they will oppose until end of time. There is no danger of revolution so great as that created by suppression, by ruthlessness, and by deliberate violation of the simple rules of American law and American decency.

It is a fallacy to suppose that, any more than in the past, any servant of the people can safely arrogate to himself unlimited authority.   To proceed upon such a supposition is to deny the fundamental American theory of the consent of the governed. Here is no question of a vague and threatened menace, but a present assault upon the most sacred principles of our Constitutional liberty.

The foregoing report has been prepared May, 1920, under the auspices of the National Popular Government League, Washington, D. C.

> R. G. BROWN, Memphis, Tenn.
> ZECHERIAH CHAFEE, JR., Cambridge, Mass.
> FELIX FRANKFURTER, Cambridge, Mass.
> ERNST FREUND, Chicago, Ill.
> SWINBURNE HALE, New York, City
> FRANCIS FISHER KANE, Philadelphia, Pa.
> ALFRED S. NILES, Baltimore, Md.
> ROSCOE POUND, Cambridge, Mass.
> JACKSON H. RALSTON, Washington, D. C.
> DAVID WALLERSTEIN, Philadelphia, Pa.
> FRANK P. WALSH, New York City.
> TYRRELL WILLIAMS, St. Louis, Mo.

The raids were particularly intense and violent in the industrial towns round Boston and culminated in the captives being driven through the streets of Boston chained together in fours.   There were raids in Boston, Chelsea, Brockton, Bridgewater, Norwood, Worcester, Springfield, Chicopee Falls, Lowell, Fitchburg, Holyoke, Lawrence and Haverhill.   Unfortunate people after being beaten up and put through the third degree were concentrated at Deer Island under the conditions that have become public through U. S. Circuit Judge Anderson's decision on the cases that came up before him.

Now it is this ring of industrial towns round Boston that furnish the background of the Sacco-Vanzetti case.   There is no doubt that the American born public in these towns on the whole sympathizes with the activities of the detectives.   The region has been for many years one of the most intense industrial battlegrounds in the country.   People slept safer in their beds at the thought of all these agitators, bombsters, garlic-smelling wops, and unwashed Russians being under lock and key at Deer Island.

Eastern Massachusetts has a threefold population living largely from manufacturing of textiles and shoes and other leather goods. With the decline of shipping and farming the old simonpure New England stock, Congregationalist in faith, Republican in politics, has been pretty well snowed under by the immigration first of Irish Catholics, congenital Democrats and readers of Hearst papers, now assimilated and respectable, and then of Italians, Poles, Slovaks, transplanted European peasants tenderly known to newspaper readers as the scum of the Mediterranean or the scum of Central Europe. There's no love lost between the first two classes, but they unite on the question of wops, guineas, dagoes. The January raids, the attitude of press and pulpit, howling about atrocities, civilization (which usually means bank accounts) endangered, women nationalized, put the average right-thinking citizen into such a state of mind that whenever he smelt garlic on a man's breath he walked past quickly for fear of being knifed. A roomful of people talking a foreign language was most certainly a conspiracy to overturn the Government. Read over the articles in the *Boston Transcript* on the soviet conspiracy at that time and you will see what kind of stuff was being ladled out even to the intelligent highbrow section of the entrenched classes.

It was into this atmosphere of rancor and suspicion, fear of holdups and social overturn that burst the scare headlines of the South Braintree murders. Pent-up hatred found an outlet when the police in Brockton arrested Sacco and Vanzetti, wops who spoke broken English, anarchists who believed neither in the Pope nor in the Puritan God, slackers and agitators, charged with a peculiarly brutal and impudent crime. Since that moment these people have had a focus for their bitter hatred of the new, young, vigorous, unfamiliar forces that are relentlessly sweeping them on to the shelf. The people of Norfolk county and of all Massachusetts decided they wanted these men to die.

Meanwhile the red delirium over the rest of the country had slackened. Something had happened that had made many people pause and think.

About dawn on May 3rd the body of Andrea Salsedo, an anarchist printer, was found smashed on the pavement of Park Row in New York. He had jumped or been thrown from the offices of the Department of Justice on the fourteenth floor of the Park Row building, where he and his friend Elia had been secretly imprisoned for eight weeks. Evidently they had continually tortured him during that time; Mr. Palmer's detectives were "investigating" anarchist activity. A note had been smuggled out somehow, and a few days before Vanzetti had been in New York as the delegate of an Italian group to try to get the two men out on bail. After Salsedo's death Elia was hurried over to Ellis Island and deported. He died in Italy. But from that time on the holy enthusiasm for red-baiting subsided. That tortured body found dead and bleeding in one of the most central and public spots in New York shocked men back into their senses.

When Sacco and Vanzetti were arrested in the trolley car in Brockton the night of May 5th, Sacco had in his pocket the draft of a poster announcing a meeting of protest against what they considered the murder of their comrade. They were going about warning the other members of their group to hide all incriminating evidence in the way of "radical" books and papers so that, in the new raid that they had been tipped off to expect, they should not be arrested and meet the fate of Salsedo.

Don't forget that people had been arrested and beaten up for distributing the Declaration of Independence.

IV

THE PSYCHOLOGY OF FRAME-UPS

But why were these men held as murderers and highwaymen and not as anarchists and advocates of the working people?

It was a frameup.

That does not *necessarily* mean that any set of government and employing class detectives deliberately planned to fasten the crime of murder on Sacco and Vanzetti. Though in this case it is almost certain that they did.

The frameup is an unconscious (occasionally semiconscious) mechanism. An unconscious mechanism is a kink in the mind that makes people do something without knowing why they do it, and often without knowing that they are doing it. It is the sub-rational act of a group, serving in this case, through a series of pointed unintentions, the ends of a governing class.

Among a people that does not recognize or rather does not admit the force and danger of ideas it is impossible to prosecute the holder of unpopular ideas directly. Also there is a smouldering tradition of freedom that makes those who do it feel guilty. After all everyone learnt the Declaration of Independence and *Give me Liberty or Give me Death* in school, and however perfunctory the words have become they have left a faint infantile impression on the minds of most of us. Hence the characteristic American weapon of the frameup. If a cop wants to arrest a man he suspects of selling dope he plants a gun on him and arrests him under the Sullivan Law. If a man is organizing a strike in a dangerously lively way you try to frame him under the Mann Act or else you get hold of a woman to sue him for breach of promise. If a representative votes against war you have him arrested for breach of decency in an automobile on a Virginia roadside. If two Italians are spreading anarchist propaganda, you hold them for murder.

The frameup is a process that you can't help feeling, but like most unconscious processes it's very hard to trace step by step. Half the agents in such a process don't really know what they are doing. Hence the average moderately fairminded newspaper reader who never has had personal experience of a frameup in action is flabbergasted when you tell him that such and such a man who is being prosecuted for wifebeating is really being prosecuted because he knows the origin of certain bonds in a District Attorney's safe.

In this neatly swept courtroom in Dedham with everything so varnished and genteel it is hardly possible to think of such a thing as a frameup, and yet... Under these elms, in these white oldtime houses of Dedham, in front of these pious Georgian doorways... The court has for the seventh time affirmed its will to send two innocent men to the electric chair.

V

THE OUTLAW CREED

But what is this criminal garlic-smelling creed that the people of Massachusetts will not face openly?

For half a century Anarchy has been the bogy of American schoolmasters, policemen, old maids, and small town mayors. About the time of the assassination of McKinley a picture was formed in the public mind of the anarchist; redhanded, unwashed foreigner whom nobody could understand, sticks of dynamite in his pocket and bomb in the paper parcel under his arm, redeyed housewrecker waiting only for the opportunity to bite the hand that fed him. Since the Russian Revolution the picture has merged a little with that of the sneaking, slinking, communist Jew, enviously undermining Prosperity and Decency through secret organizations ruled from Moscow.

Gradually among liberals and intelligent people generally certain phases of anarchism have meanwhile been reluctantly admitted into respectable conversation under the phrase 'philosophical anarchist', which means an anarchist who shaves daily, has good manners and is guaranteed not to act on his beliefs. Certain people of the best society, such as Kropotkin and Tolstoy, princes both, having through their anarchy made themselves important figures in European thought and literature, it was impossible to exclude them longer from the pale of decency.

What is this outlaw creed?

When Christianity flourished in the Mediterranean basin, slave and emperor had the hope of the immediate coming of Christ's kingdom, the golden Jerusalem that would appear on earth to put an end to the tears and aches of the faithful. After the first millennium, the City of God, despaired of on earth, took its permanent place in the cloudy firmament with the Virgin Mary at the apex of the feudal pyramid. With the decay of feudalism and the coming of the kingdoms of this world the church became more and more the instrument of the governing orders. Undermined by the eighteenth century, overthrown by the French revolution, the church was restored by the great reaction as the strongest bulwark of Privilege. But in the tough memories of peasants and fishermen—their sons worked in factories—there remained a faint trace of the vanished brightness of the City of God. All our citydwelling instinct and culture has been handed down to us from these countless urban generations, Cretans, Greeks, Phoenicians, Latins of the Mediterranean basin, Italians of the hilltowns. It is natural that the dwellers on those scraggy hills in sight of that always blue sea should have kept alight in their hearts the perfect city, where the strong did not oppress the weak, where every man lived by his own work at peace with his neighbors, the white Commune where man could reach his full height free from the old snarling obsessions of god and master.

It is this inner picture that is the core of feeling behind all anarchist theory and doctrine. Many Italians planted the perfect city of their imagination in America. When they came to this country they either killed the perfect city in their hearts and submitted to the system of dawg eat dawg or else they found themselves anarchists. There have been terrorists among them, as in every other oppressed and despised sect since the world began. Good people generally have contended that anarchism and terrorism were the same thing, a silly and usually malicious error much fostered by private detectives and the police bomb-squads.

An anarchist workman who works for the organization of his fellow workmen is a man who costs the factory owners money; thereby he is a bomb-thrower and possible murderer in the minds of the majority of American employers.

In his charge to the jury in the Plymouth trial Judge Thayer definitely said that the crime of highway robbery was consistent with Vanzetti's ideals as a radical.

Yet under the conflict between employer and workman, and the racial misunderstanding, in themselves material enough for the creation of a frameup, might there not be a deeper bitterness? The people of Massachusetts centuries ago suffered and hoped terribly for the City of God. This little white courthouse town of Dedham, neat and exquisite under its elms, is the symbol of a withered hope, mortgaged at six per cent to the kingdoms of this world. It is natural that New Englanders, who feel in themselves a lingering of the passionate barbed desire of perfection of their ancestors, should hate with particular bitterness, anarchists, votaries of the Perfect Commune on earth. The irrational features of this case of attempted communal murder can only be explained by a bitterness so deep that it has been forgotten by the very people it moves most fervidly.

VI

FREE MEN

It was about dawn on Monday, May 3rd, 1920, that the body of Andrea Salsedo was found smashed on the pavement of Park Row. At that time Bartolomeo Vanzetti was peddling fish in the pleasant little Italian and Portuguese town of North Plymouth. He was planning to go into fishing himself in partnership with a man who owned some dories. Early mornings, pushing his cart up and down the long main street, ringing his bell, chatting with housewives in Piedmontese, Tuscan, pidgin English, he worried about the raids, the imprisonment of comrades, the lethargy of the working people. He was an anarchist, after the school of Galleani. Between the houses he could see the gleaming stretch of Plymouth Bay, the sandy islands beyond, the white dories at anchor. About three hundred years before, men from the west of England had first sailed into the grey shimmering bay that smelt of woods and wild grape, looking for something; liberty.... freedom to worship God in their own manner.... space to breathe. Thinking of these things, worrying as he pushed the little cart loaded with eels, haddock, cod, halibut, swordfish, Vanzetti spent his mornings making change, weighing out fish, joking with the housewives. It was better than working at the great cordage works that own North Plymouth. Some years before he had tried to organize a strike there and been blacklisted. The officials and detectives at the Plymouth Cordage Works, the largest cordage works in the world, thought of him as a Red, a slacker and troublemaker.

His life up to his settling in Plymouth you can read in his own words in these extracts from the *Story of a Proletarian Life* that he wrote in Charlestown jail:

My life cannot claim the dignity of an autobiography. Nameless, in the crowd of nameless ones, I have merely caught and reflected a little of the light from that dynamic thought or ideal which is drawing humanity towards better destinies.

I was born on June 11, 1888, of G. Battista Vanzetti and Giovanna Vanzetti, in Villafalletto, province of Cuneo, in Piedmont. The town, which rises on the right bank of the Magra, in the shadows of a beautiful chain of hills, is primarily an agricultural community. Here I lived until the age of thirteen in the bosom of my family.

I attended the local schools and loved study. My earliest memories are of prizes won in school examinations, including a second prize in the religious catechism. My father was undecided whether to let me prosecute studies or to apprentice me to some artisan. One day he read in the *Gazzetta del Popolo* that in Turin forty-two lawyers had applied for a position paying 35 lire monthly. The news item proved decisive in my boyhood, for it left my father determined that I should learn a trade and become a shop keeper.

And so in the year 1901 he conducted me to Signor Conino, who ran a pastry shop in the city of Cuneo, and left me there to taste, for the first time, the flavor of hard, relentless labor. I worked for about twenty months there—from seven o'clock each morning until ten at night, every day, except for a three-hour vacation twice a month. From Cuneo I went to Cavour and found myself installed in the bakery of Signor Goitre, a place that I kept for three years. Conditions were no better than in Cuneo, except that the fortnightly free period was of five hours duration.

I did not like the trade, but I stuck to it to please my father and because I did not know what else to choose. In 1905 I abandoned Cavour for Turin in the hope of locating work in the big city. Failing in this hope, I went on further to Courgne where I remained working six months. Then back to Turin, on a job as caramel-maker.

In Turin, in February of 1907, I fell seriously ill. I was in great pain, confined indoors, deprived of air and sun and joy, like a "sad twilight flower." But news of my plight reached the family and my father came from Villafalletto to take me back

to my birthplace.   At home, he told me, I would be cared for
by my mother, my good, my best-beloved mother.

*   *   *   *   *   *   *   *

Science did not avail, nor love.   After three months of
brutal illness she breathed her last in my arms.   She died
without hearing me weep.   It was I who laid her in her coffin;
I who accompanied her to the final resting place; I who threw
the first handful of earth over her bier.   And it was right that
I should do so, for I was burying part of myself... The void
left has never been filled.

*   *   *   *   *   *   *   *

This desperate state of mind decided me to abandon Italy
for America.   On June 9, 1908, I left my dear ones.   My sorrow
was so great at the parting that I kissed my relatives and
strained them to my bosom without being able to speak.   My
father, too, was speechless in his profound sorrow, and my
sisters wept as they did when my mother died.   My going had
excited interest in the village and the neighbors crowded the
house, each with a word of hope, a blessing, a tear.   In a crowd
they followed me far out on the road, as if a townsman were
being exiled forever.

*   *   *   *   *   *   *   *

After a two-day railway ride across France and more than
seven days on the ocean, I arrived in the Promised Land.   New
York loomed on the horizon in all its grandness and illusion of
happiness.   I strained my eyes from the steerage deck, trying to
see through this mass of masonry that was at once inviting and
threatening to the huddled men and women in the third class.

In the immigration station I had my first great surprise.
I saw the steerage passengers handled by the officials like so
many animals.   Not a word of kindness, of encouragement, to
lighten the burden of fears that rests heavily upon the newly
arrived on American shores.   Hope, which lured these immigrants to the new land, withers under the touch of harsh
officials.   Little children who should be alert with expectancy,
cling instead to their mothers' skirts, weeping with fright.
Such is the unfriendly spirit that exists in the immigration
barracks.

How well I remember standing at the Battery, in lower New
York, upon my arrival, alone, with a few poor belongings in the
way of clothes, and very little money.   Until yesterday I was
among folks who understood me.   This morning I seemed to
have awakened in a land where my language meant little more to
the native (so far as meaning is concerned) than the pitiful

noises of a dumb animal. Where was I to go? What was I to do? Here was the promised land. The elevated rattled by and did not answer. The automobiles and the trolleys speed by, heedless of me.

I had note of one address, and thither a fellow-passenger conducted me. It was the house of a countryman of mine, on —street, near Seventh Avenue. I remained there a while, but it became all too evident that there was no room for me in his house, which was overstocked with human beings, like all workingmen's houses. In deep melancholy I left the place towards eight in the evening to look for a place to sleep. I retraced my steps to the Battery, where I took a bed for the night in a suspicious-looking establishment, the best I could afford. Three days after my arrival, the compatriot already mentioned, who was head cook in a rich club on West —— street overlooking the Hudson River, found me a post in his kitchen as dishwasher. I worked there three months. The hours were long; the garret where we slept was suffocatingly hot; and the vermin did not permit me to close an eye. Almost every night I sought escape in the park.

Leaving this place, I found the same kind of employment in the Mouquin Restaurant. What the conditions there are at present I do not know. But at that time, thirteen years ago, the pantry was horrible. There was not a single window in it. When the electric light for some reason was out, it was totally dark, so that one couldn't move without running into things. The vapor of the boiling water where the plates, pans and silver were washed formed great drops of water on the ceiling, took up all the dust and grime there, then fell slowly one by one upon my head, as I worked below. During working hours the heat was terrific. The table leavings amassed in barrels near the pantry gave out nauseating exhalations. The sinks had no direct sewerage connection. Instead, the water was permitted to overrun to the floor. In the center of the room there was a drain. Every night the pipe was clogged and the greasy water rose higher and higher and we trudged in the slime.

We worked twelve hours one day and fourteen the next, with five hours off every Sunday. Damp food hardly fit for dogs and five or six dollars a week was the pay. After eight months I left the place for fear of contracting consumption.

That was a sad year. What toiler does not remember it? The poor slept outdoors and rummaged the garbage barrels to find a cabbage leaf or a rotten potato. For three months I searched New York, its length and its breadth, without finding work. One morning, in an employment agency, I meet a young

man more forlorn and unfortunate than I. He had gone without food the day before and was still fasting. I took him to a
restaurant, investing almost all that remained to me of my
savings in a meal which he ate with wolfish voracity. His
hunger stilled, my new friend declared that it was stupid to
remain in New York. If he had the money, he said, he would go
to the country, where there was more chance of work, without
counting the pure air and the sun which could be had for
nothing. With the money remaining in my possession we took
the steamboat for Hartford, Connecticut, the same day.

*   *   *   *   *   *   *   *

From Worcester I transferred to Plymouth (that was about
seven years ago), which remained my home until the time I
was arrested. I learned to look upon the place with a real
affection, because as time went on it held more and more of
the people dear to my heart, the folks I boarded with, the men
who worked by my side, the women who later bought the wares
I had to offer as a peddler.

In passing, let me say how gratifying it is to realize that
my compatriots in Plymouth reciprocate the love I feel for them.
Not only have they supported my defense—money is a slight
thing after all—but they have expressed to me directly and
indirectly their faith in my innocence. Those who rallied around
my good friends of the defense committee, were not only
workers, but businessmen who knew me; not only Italians, but
Jews, Poles, Greeks and Americans.

Well, I worked in the Stone establishment for more than
a year, and then for the Cordage Company for about eighteen
months. My active participation in the Plymouth cordage strike
made it certain that I could never get a job there..... As a
matter of fact, because of my more frequent appearance on the
speaker's platform in working class groups of every kind, it
became increasingly difficult to get work anywhere. So far as
certain factories were concerned I was definitely "blacklisted."
Yet, every one of my many employers could testify that I was
an industrious, dependable workman, that my chief fault was
in trying so hard to bring a little light of understanding into
the dark lives of my fellow-workers. For some time I did
manual work of the hardest kind in the construction under-
takings of Sampson & Douland, for the city. I can almost say
that I have participated in all the principal public works in
Plymouth. Almost any Italian in the town or any of my foremen
of my various jobs can attest my industry and modesty of life
during this period. I was deeply interested by this time in the
things of the intellect, in the great hope that animates me even

here in the dark cell of a prison while I await death for a crime I did not commit.

My health was not good. The years of toil and the more terrible periods of unemployment had robbed me of much of my original vitality. I was casting about for some salutary means of eking out my livelihood. About eight months before my arrest a friend of mine who was planning to return to the home country said to me: "Why don't you buy my cart, my knives, my scales, and go to selling fish instead of remaining under the yoke of the bosses?" I grasped the opportunity, and so became a fish-vender, largely out of love for independence.

At that time, 1919, the desire to see once more my dear ones at home, the nostalgia for my native land had entered my heart. My father, who never wrote a letter without inviting me home, insisted more than ever, and my good sister Luigia joined in his pleas. Business was none too fat, but I worked like a beast of burden, without halt or stay, day after day.

December 24, the day before Christmas, was the last day I sold fish that year. A brisk day of business I had, since all Italians buy eels that day for the Christmas Eve feasts. Readers may recall that it was a bitter-cold Christmas, and the harsh weather did not let up after the holidays; and pushing a cart along is not warming work. I went for a short period to more vigorous, even if no less freezing work. I got a job a few days after Christmas cutting ice for Mr. Petersani. One day, when he hadn't enough to go round, I shovelled coal for the Electric House. When the ice job was finished I got employment with Mr. Howland, ditch-digging, until a snow storm made me a man of leisure again. Not for longer than a few hours. I hired myself out to the town, cleaning the streets of the snow, and this work done, I helped clean the snow from the railroad tracks. Then I was taken on again by the Sampson Construction people who were laying a water main for the Puritan Woolen Company. I stayed on the job until it was finished.

Again I found no job. The railroad strike difficulties had cut off the cement supply, so that there was no more construction work going on. I went back to my fish-selling, when I could get none, I dug for clams, but the profit on these was lilliputian, the expenses being so high that they left no margin. In April I reached an agreement with a fisherman for a partnership. It never materialized, because on May 5, while I was preparing a mass meeting to protest against the death of Salsedo at the hands of the Department of Justice, I was arrested. My good friend and comrade Nicola Sacco was with me.

"Another deportation case," we said to one another.

*   *   *   *   *   *   *   *

At the same time Nicola Sacco was living in Stoughton, working an edging machine at the Three K's shoe factory, where star workmen sometimes make as high as eighty or ninety dollars a week. He had a pretty wife and a little son named Dante. There was another baby coming. He lived in a bungalow belonging to his employer, Michael Kelly. The house adjoined Kelly's own house and the men were friends. Often Kelly advised him to lay off this anarchist stuff. There was no money in it. It was dangerous the way people felt nowadays. Sacco was a clever young fellow and could soon get to be a prosperous citizen, maybe own a factory of his own some day, live by other men's work. But Sacco working in his garden in the early morning before the whistles blew, hilling beans, picking off potatobugs, letting grains of corn slip by threes or fours through his fingers into the finely worked earth, worried about things. He was an anarchist. He loved the earth and people, he wanted them to walk straight over the free hills, not to stagger bowed under the ordained machinery of industry; he worried mornings working in his garden at the lethargy of the working people. It was not enough that he was happy and had fifteen hundred or more dollars in the bank for a trip home to Italy.

Two men sitting on a bench in the bright birdcage of Dedham jail. When he wants to, one of them will get up and go out, walk along the street, turn his nose into the wind, look up at the sky and clouds, board streetcars, buy train tickets. The other will go back to his cell. Twentythree hours a day in a cell for a thousand days, for three years, for six years, now the seventh year is tediously unreeling... Sacco in prisonclothes, with the prison pallor under the black hair on his head, with the prison strain under his eyes, in grey baggy prison clothes, telling about his life in the unimaginable days when he was free. A bell rings; the prisoners file by to the messroom, putty faces, slouched bodies in baggy grey denim, their hands tucked under their folded arms... Sacco was born in Torremaggiore in the province of Foggia in the sunny southern foothills of the Appenines; his father was a substantial Italian peasant who married the daughter of an oil and wine merchant. His father belonged to the republican club of the town, his older brother Sabino was a socialist. He went to school and worked in his father's vineyards and helped with the olive oil business. His oldest brother Nicola (whose name he afterwards took; when a child he was known as Ferdinando) died, Sabino was conscripted into the army; that left him the head of the family. He was often sent round the country in a cart to make payments for his father, to pay off workmen or buy supplies. He was the trusted boy of the family. But better than anything he liked machines. Summers when there was nothing that needed doing in the vineyard he worked stoking the big steam threshing machine that threshed all the wheat of the region. Better than school or farming or working for his father he liked working round engines. He dreamed about going to America, the land of engines.

When he was seventeen he set out with his brother Sabino; they were going to make their fortunes in the land of machines and dollars. In April 1908 they landed in Boston. Sacco had good luck. He worked hard. He hadn't been in this country two weeks before he had a job as waterboy with a road gang near Milford. He liked it especially when the engineer let him help with the steam roller. He liked to stand beside the hot wheezing petulant engine, stoking it with coal, squirting oil out of an oilcan. But there wasn't much money in it; winter came on. He got a job in the Hopedale mills trimming the slag off pigiron. He worked there a year. By that time he realized that he ought to learn a definite trade. An unskilled laborer was a mat for everybody to wipe their feet on. He paid fifty dollars to a man to teach him to run an edging machine. A friend of his worked as an edger in a shoefactory and made good money. That way he would have a machine all to himself.

About that time his brother Sabino had gone back to Italy, to the oil and wine business; he had had enough of America. Nicola wanted to stay on some more. First he got a job in a shoefactory in Webster, but then he went back to Milford where he worked as an edger till 1917. If he hadn't met his wife he would have gone home. At that time he was a socialist interested in *Il Proletario* a paper that Giovannitti edited, fond of acting

plays with titles like *Senza Padrone, Tempeste Sociali*. It was
at a dance he had gotten up as a benefit for an old accordeon
player who was paralyzed, that he first met Rosa his wife. She
won a box of candy in the raffle. She was from the north of
Italy and had the dark auburn hair Lombard women are famous
for. They married and were very happy; a son was born to
them whom they named Dante.

Towards 1913 Sacco began to go around to an anarchist
club, the Circolo di Studi Sociali. He found the men there more
intelligent, more anxious to read, more willing to work for the
education of their fellow workers. In 1916 the group held
manifestations of sympathy and collected money to help the
strike Carlo Tresca was running in Minnesota. The Milford
police forbade the meetings and arrested the speakers. Sacco
was among them. They were convicted in Milford for disturbing
the peace, but discharged before a superior court in Worcester.

Those were exciting years, full of the rumblings of revolution. The successful seizure of power by the Bolsheviki in
Russia made it seem that the war would end in universal
revolution. Then Mr. Wilson began his great crusade. In May
1917, with several friends, Sacco went south to Mexico to avoid
registering for the draft. It was on the train he first met Vanzetti.

When he came back from Mexico three months later he
worked in a candy factory in Cambridge, then in East Boston
and at last moved out to Stoughton, where he was a trusted man
in the Three K's Factory of the Kellys.

Sacco before his arrest was unusually powerfully built, able
to do two men's work. In prison he was able to stand thirtyone
days of hunger strike before he broke down and had to be taken
to the hospital. In prison he has learned to speak and write
English, has read many books, for the first time in his life has
been thrown with nativeborn Americans. They are so hard and
brittle. They don't fit into the bright clear heartfelt philosophy
of Latin anarchism. These are the people who cooly want him
to die in the electric chair. He can't understand them. When
his head was cool he's never wanted anyone to die. Judge Thayer
and the prosecution he thinks of as instruments of a machine.

VII

SLACKERS, REDS

Three years before Sacco and Vanzetti had both of them had their convictions put to the test. In 1917, against the expressed votes of the majority, Woodrow Wilson had allowed the United States to become involved in the war with Germany. When the law was passed for compulsory military service a registration day for citizens and aliens was announced. Most young men submitted whatever their convictions were. A few of those who were morally opposed to any war or to capitalist war had the nerve to protest. Sacco and Vanzetti and some friends ran away to Mexico. There, some thirty of them lived in a set of adobe houses. Those who could get jobs worked. It was share and share alike. Everything was held in common. There were in the community men of all trades and conditions; bakers, butchers, tailors, shoemakers, cooks, carpenters, waiters. Sacco got a job in a bakery and when the others were hard up would take his pay in bread. Saturday nights he'd trudge home to the community with a bag of fresh loaves of bread over his shoulder. It was a momentary realization of the hope of anarchism. But living was difficult in Mexico and they began to get letters from the States telling that it was possible to avoid the draft, telling of high wages. Little by little they filtred back across the border. Sacco and Vanzetti went back to Massachusetts.

There was an Italian club that met Sunday evenings in a hall in Maverick Square, East Boston, under the name of the Italian Naturalization Club. Workmen from the surrounding industrial towns met to play bowls and discuss social problems. There were anarchists, syndicalists, socialists of various colors. The Russian revolution had fired them with new hopes. The persecution of their comrades in various parts of America had made them feel the need for mutual help. While far away across the world new eras seemed to be flaring up into the sky, at home the great machine they slaved for seemed more adamant, more unshakable than ever. Everywhere aliens were being arrested, tortured, deported. To the war heroes who had remained at home any foreigner seemed a potential Bolshevik, a menace to the security of Old Glory and liberty bonds and the bonus. When Elia and Salsedo were arrested in New York there was great alarm among the Italian radicals around Boston. Vanzetti went down to New York to try to hire a lawyer for the two men. There he heard many uneasy rumors. The possession of any literature that might be interpreted as subversive by ignorant and brutal agents of the departments of Justice and Labor was dangerous. It was not that deportation was so much to be feared, but the beating up and third degree that preceded it.

On the evening of May 5th, Sacco and Vanzetti with the handbill on them announcing a meeting of protest against what they considered the murder of Salsedo, went by trolley from Stoughton to West Bridgewater to meet a man named Boda who they thought could lend them a car. Very likely they thought they were being trailed and had put revolvers in their pockets out of some confused feeling of bravado. If the police pounced on them at least they would not let themselves be tortured to death like Salsedo. But they were afraid to use Boda's car because it lacked a 1920 license plate and started back to Stoughton on the trolley, probably very uneasy. When they were arrested as the trolley entered Brockton they forgot all about their guns. They thought they were being arrested as Reds in connection with the projected meeting. When they were questioned at the police station their main care was not to implicate any of their friends. They kept remembering the dead body of Salsedo, smashed on the pavement of Park Row.

VIII

JAILBIRDS

The faces of men who have been a long time in jail have a peculiar frozen look under the eyes. The face of a man who has been a long time in jail never loses that tightness under the eyes. Sacco has been six years in the county jail, alway waiting, waiting for trial, waiting for new evidence, waiting for motions to be argued, waiting for sentence, waiting, waiting, waiting. The Dedham jail is a handsome structure, set among lawns, screened by trees that wave new green leaves against the robinsegg sky of June. In the warden's office you can see your face in the light brown varnish, you could eat eggs off the floor it is so clean. Inside the main reception hall is airy, full of sunlight. The bars are bright with reflected spring greens, a fresh peagreen light is over everything. Through the bars you can see the waving trees and the June clouds roaming the sky like cattle in an unfenced pasture. It's a preposterous complicated canary cage. Why aren't the birds singing in this green aviary? The warden politely shows you a seat and as you wait you notice a smell, not green and airy this smell, a jaded heavy greasy smell of slum, like the smell of army slum, but heavier, more hopeless.

Across the hall an old man is sitting in a chair, a heavy pear-shaped man, his hands limp at his sides, his eyes are closed, his sagged face is like a bundle of wet newspapers. The warden and two men in black stand over him, looking down at him helplessly.

At last Sacco has come out of his cell and sits beside me. Two men sitting side by side on a bench in a green, bird cage. When he feels like it one of them will get up and walk out, walk out into the sunny June day. The other will go back to his cell to wait. He looks younger than I had expected. His face has a waxy transparency like the face of a man who's been sick in bed for long time; when he laughs his cheeks flush a little. At length we manage both of us to laugh. It's such a preposterous position for a man to be in, like a man who doesn't know the game trying to play chess blindfolded. The real world has gone. We have no more grasp of our world of rain and streets and trolleycars and cucumbervines and girls and gardenplots. This is a world of phrases, *prosecution, defence, evidence, motion, irrelevant, incompetent and immaterial.* For six years this man has lived in the law, tied tighter and tighter in the sticky filaments of law-words like a fly in a spiderweb. And the wrong set of words means the Chair. All the moves in the game are made for him, all he can do is sit helpless and wait, fastening his hopes on one set of phrases after another. In all these lawbooks, in all this terminology of clerks of the court and counsel for the defence there is one move that will save him, out of a million that will mean death. If only they make the right move, use the right words. But by this time the nagging torment of hope has almost stopped, not even the thought of his wife and children out there in the world, unreachable, can torture him now. He is numb now, can laugh and look quizzically at the ponderous machine that has caught and mangled him. Now it hardly matters to him if they do manage to pull him out from between the cogs, and the wrong set of words means the Chair.

The warden comes up to take down my name. "I hope your wife's better," says Sacco. "Pretty poorly," says the warden. Sacco shakes his head. "Maybe she'll get better soon, nice weather." I have shaken his hand, my feet have carried me to the door, past the baggy pearshaped man who is still collapsed half deflated in the chair, closed crinkled eyelids twitching. The warden looks into my face with a curious smile, "Leaving us?" he asks. Outside in the neat streets the new green leaves are swaying in the sunlight, birds sing, klaxons grunt, a trolleycar screeches round a corner. Overhead the white June clouds wander in the unfenced sky.

Going to the State Prison at Charlestown is more like going to Barnum and Baileys. There's a great scurry of guards, groups of people waiting outside; inside a brass band is playing *Home Sweet Home.*   When at length you get let into the Big Show, you find a great many things happening at once. There are rows of chairs where pairs of people sit talking. Each pair is made up of a free man and a convict.   In three directions there are grey bars and tiers of cells. The band inside plays bangingly "If Auld Acquaintance Be Forgot." A short broad-shouldered man is sitting quiet through all the uproar, smiling a little under his big drooping mustache. He has a domed, pale forehead and black eyes surrounded by many little wrinkles. The serene modeling of his cheek-bones and hollow cheeks makes you forget the prison look under his eyes.

This is Vanzetti.

And for the last six years, three hundred and sixtyfive days a year, yesterday, today, tomorrow, Sacco and Vanzetti wake up on their prison pallets, eat prison food, have an hour of exercise and conversation a day, sit in their cells puzzling about this technicality and that technicality, pinning their hopes to their alibis, to the expert testimony about the character of the barrel of Sacco's gun, to Madeiros' confession and Weeks' corroboration, to action before the Supreme Court of the United States, and day by day the props are dashed from under their feet and they feel themselves being inexorably pushed towards the Chair by the blind hatred of thousands of wellmeaning citizens, by the superhuman, involved, stealthy, soulless mechanism of the law.

IX

THE PLYMOUTH TRIAL OF VANZETTI ALONE

"But Vanzetti had a criminal record", they tell you, "he was serving a jail sentence when he was brought up for trial with Sacco."

This is the story of Vanzetti's criminal record.

In 1914 Vanzetti had a job loading rope coils on freightcars with the outside gang of the Plymouth Cordage. The Plymouth Cordage is the largest in the world, and virtually owns Plymouth and the surrounding towns where colonies of Italians and Portuguese worked (at that time for a maximum of nine dollars a week) tending the spinning machines that transform hemp shipped up from Yucatan into rope and binder twine. On January 17, 1916, there was a big walkout, the first in the history of the Cordage. Vanzetti was one of the organizers of the strike. After the plant had been shut down for a month in the busiest season, the company conceded a raise. Since then wages have risen to round twenty five a week. Vanzetti was always in the front, picketing, making speeches. He was the only employee who did not get his job back when the strike was settled.

At the time of the arrest of Sacco and Vanzetti there was a general impression that the gunmen in a Buick car who attempted to hold up a paytruck of the L. Q. White company in Bridgewater on the morning of day before Christmas 1919, were Italians and the same as those who had made off with the South Braintree payroll.

It was impossible to implicate Sacco in that affair as he had been working that day. Vanzetti was his own boss, so he could not give himself a certificate of employment. He was taken over to Plymouth and brought to trial under Judge Thayer in June, Mr. Katzmann prosecuting the case for the state. It is very probable that the man hired to defend Vanzetti deliberately gave away his client's case. In any event he showed criminal negligence in neglecting to file a bill of exceptions and in refusing to allow Vanzetti to take the stand in his own defence.

This is what Vanzetti himself says about it in a letter to some friends in Mexico:

"As for Mr. Vahey, he had asked me very little concerning my defence, and, from after the preliminary hearing to the end of the trial, he did not put to me a single new question about the case. On the contrary, he began to promise me the electric chair. 'They will put you with Sacco', and... at this point he used to cease to speak, to begin to whistle, tracing upward spiral motions with his right hand, its index finger straight up. This is the sole Herculean fatigue accomplished by Mr. Vahey in my defence, while smoking big cigars bought him by the poor Italian people. But Mr. Vahey's words proved that he knew before the Plymouth trial that I would be indicted for the Braintree robbery and slaying * * *   To suppose that Mr. Vahey and his agent Govoni might have been induced to such conduct by their conviction of my guilt, would be as wrong as it is unjust. There had been nothing in the case to justify, not even to excuse, such a doubt. I have always protested my innocence; the Italian population and some Americans of Plymouth had run in a mass to prove it. The preliminary hearing had proved the impossibility and inconsistency of the charge against me as the record shows. The truth is that both the prosecution and the defence counsel had realized that without the latter's betrayal the frame-up in the making would have been an utter failure; hence the betrayal."

The Bridgewater holdup had occurred at 7.35 A. M. It was an armed attack on three occupants of the L. Q. White Shoe Company's paytruck. This truck had obtained the weekly allotment of money for White's, said to be $33,000, at a bank in the public square, and was on its way to the shoe factory.

Its route lay northward on Broad Street, along which a trolley track runs. One block north of the public square, Hale Street, a narrow lane, cuts into Broad Street from the east, and ends there. One block farther north there are railroad tracks and a depot, the latter being set back considerably from Broad Street to the east, so that it cannot be seen from the crime-zone.

As the paytruck approached Hale Street, two men on foot began firing at the three on board—a paymaster, a special officer, and a chauffeur. The fire was returned. One bandit had a revolver, and the other a shotgun. Later Vanzetti was declared to be the shotgun man. The truck escaped around a trolleycar.

No one was injured, nor were any bullet marks afterwards found. The bandits jumped into an automobile which waited with engine running in Hale street, and fled.

At that hour Vanzetti was actually 28 miles away—in Plymouth, where he was well known as a fishseller. December 24th stands out always on the Italian calendar. Among the Catholics it is a fast day, and fish is the logical food. But the feasting spirit of the Christmas-tide is in the air, and the fish of ordinary days is not rich enough, so the Italians eat eels.

Vanzetti had taken orders in advance from numerous families for eels. On the evening of December 23rd, he arranged with thirteen-year-old Bertrando Brini to have him help in the delivery of the eels. Next morning the two went through the streets together making those deliveries. They were seen by many people. That day stood out in Bertrando's memory because it was then he earned his Christmas money.

Eighteen reputable witnesses vouched for Vanzetti's whereabouts on that day. Nine of those had been at home when he brought the eels, and talked with him. John Di Carlo, proprietor of a shoe store, testified that Vanzetti came to his store while he was cleaning up that morning—between 7:15 and 7:40 A. M.

Every hour of Vanzetti's time that Christmas Eve was accounted for.

Those who swore that they purchased eels from him included Mrs. Mary Fortini, Mrs. Rosa Forni, Rosa Balboni, Teresa Malaguice, Adelaide Bongiovanni, Marquetta Fiochi, Emma Bosari, Enrico Bastoni, a baker, and Vincent J. Longhi.

All these are persons of good repute. Their testimony was straightforward and certain. The prosecution made no serious attempt to disprove it.

Prosecutor Katzmann, who says this is solely a criminal case, asked Di Carlo during cross-examintion:

"Have you ever discussed government theories over there between you?" and "Have you discussed the question of the poor man and the rich man between you?" (Trial record, Page 47).

And when Michael Sassi, cordage worker, was testifying for Vanzetti, the prosecutor asked: "Have you heard anything of his political speeches to fellow workers at the Cordage?"

Witnesses for the prosecution were few and inconsistent; several altered their testimony, consciously or unconsciously, to fit the prosecution's needs.

Frank W. Harding, better known as "Slip," originally described the shotgun bandit as "smooth-shaven," according to the Boston Globe of December 24, 1919. But in the official transcript of the preliminary hearing of Vanzetti on May 10, he uses five lines to describe the "overgrown Charlie Chaplin" moustache of the same man. This description was given after he had seen Vanzetti.

Similar alteration of testimony was made by Benjamin J. Bowles, one of the men on the paytruck. Bowles is a special officer for the White Shoe Company and member of Chief Stewart's police force in Bridgewater. At the preliminary hearing Bowles swore the shotgun man's moustache was "short and croppy." But presently it became known that Policemen Schilling and Gault, of Plymouth, together with the Chief of Police there and various prominent persons, would testify for the defense that Vanzetti's moustache had been full and flowing for years. So in the trial Bowles declared that the shotgun man's moustache was "bushy."

Bowles' "pretty positive" identification, thrice repeated at the preliminary hearing (Page 32, preliminary record), became "positive" in the trial. (Page 25, trial record.)

Although refusing to make a positive identification for the commonwealth, Paymaster Alfred E. Cox reversed his general testimony at the trial and gave a description which would fit the defendant. In the Brockton police court on May 10, Cox declared several times that the shotgun man, in contrast to the other bandit, was "short and of slight build" (Page 11, preliminary record), the "short" fellow of the attacking party.

This was bad for the commonwealth's case. But it didn't stand. Bowles followed Cox with a "five feet eight inches" description which fitted Vanzetti better, and said that the shotgun man was the taller of the two. Then, when the case went to trial, Bowles was called first and Cox carefully patterned his description after him and let the bandit grow taller. When Bowles again said "five feet eight inches" Cox repeated "five feet eight inches."

Bowles gave a description of the shotgun man's hair, eyes, face and clothes of minute completeness. Such fullness of detail six months after he had seen a man for only a few chaotic seconds seems incredible. Bowles described graphically how he helped operate the motor truck after Earl Graves, the driver, collapsed from fright with the first bullet, and how they steered around a trolley car directly ahead of them.

And most marvelous of all—at the very time when he was doing this, he was engaged in a pistol duel with another bandit from the one he was describing. This other bandit, he said, was fully eight feet away from the shotgun man. All this is in the preliminary trial record.

At the trial however the defense attorneys challenged Bowles on the latter point and he promptly changed his testimony, saying now that his second shot was fired at the shotgun man. But he had just said that he was from 25 to 50 yards away when he fired the second shot.

Mrs. Georgina Brooks is an elderly woman who appears to have supernatural powers. Buildings become transparent when they stand in her way. She declared she saw "fire and smoke from a gun" while she stood in a window of the railway station, 75 feet back from Broad Street and 300 feet from Hale Street where the events took place.

But there is a two-story frame house half-way along Broad Street which completely shuts off an observer in that window from any view of the crime-area!

Mrs. Brooks makes no secret of being able to see only the vague silhouette of objects before her with one of her eyes, and she has been taking treatment for the other. But on the way to the railroad station with a small child before the shooting, she took observations afterwards useful to the prosecution. She was walking north on the west side of Broad Street, she said, when she noticed an automobile drawn up in Hale street, east of the eastern sidewalk line on Broad Street. The rear of the car was toward her.

For some unexplained reason she became interested in that car, although its appearance was not unusual. She led the child across Broad Street and into Hale Street, and went out of her way to pass around the front end of the automobile. In it, she said, were four men. Three of these she took no notice of; but she scrutinized the fourth—a man with a dark face, moustache and dark soft hat, who "seemed like some kind of a foreigner."

She looked twice at this man, who in return looked at her "severely"; and she continued to turn and look at him as she and the child proceeded to the railroad station. That man, she declared, to quote from the trial record, "That man, I should judge, was the defendant."

Paymaster Cox testified at the preliminary hearing, as did Mrs. Brooks, that Vanzetti had worn a hat. But this detail given by Cox was carefully suppressed by the prosecution during the trial. Chief Stewart exhibited in court a cap, which he claimed to have taken from Vanzetti's home; then he produced a witness, Richard Grant Casey, who said he thought he saw this cap on the shotgun man's head on December 24.

Maynard Freeman Shaw, 14-year-old high school prodigy, stood behind a tree and saw the shotgun man running 145 feet away. He was one of those who "identified" Vanzetti. He admitted he never had more than a fleeting glimpse of the bandit's face.

"I could tell he was a foreigner by the way he ran," young Shaw testified at the trial.

"What sort of a foreigner?" asked the defense.

"Either Italian or Russian."

"Does an Italian or a Russian run differently from a Swede or a Norwegian?"

"Yes."

"What is the difference?"

"Unsteady."

Courtroom spectators were impressed by the heroic recital of "Slip" Harding. He described modestly his own coolness under fire; how he stood in the open during the gun-play in the Bridgewater attack. Some onlookers assert that Harding was behind a tree, but he testified that he took down the number of the bandits' automobile as it sped away. Then he gave the memorandum to Police Chief Stewart, he said, and failed to keep a copy of it.

When Stewart went on the witness stand he stated that he had mislaid that important memorandum. After spending a whole day searching for the automobile number, he had to confess that he had lost it. Later, however, he gave "from memory" a number which he asserted was that of the bandit car. That was six months after the crime. The number Stewart gave was that of a car stolen from Francis Murphy, a Natick shoe manufacturer, in November, 1919.

Two days after the South Braintree holdup, an abandoned Buick automobile, identified as Murphy's, was found several miles away. The prosecution contended that it was used in both crimes.

Vanzetti was connected with that car by the thinnest threads. Remember the three shotgun shells found in his pocket many days after the second holdup. The prosecutors tried to introduce as evidence a fourth shotgun shell, alleged to have been found alongside the automobile. Judge Thayer would not admit its introduction.

Whether that shell actually was found beside the car may be questioned, in the light of a news story in the Boston Globe of April 19. That story told of State Detective Scott and Police Chief Jeremiah Gallivan of Braintree beating the bush for the missing $15,000 payroll.

(A curious thing about the South Braintree crime is that no trace of the stolen money, or of the black boxes that were said to have contained it, has been found. Stewart had an idea it was in Coacci's trunk. It was not there. The only mention of any money that could possibly have come from that source was the two thousand dollars Madeiros went South with late in 1920. Being questioned by Mr. Thompson he refused to say where it came from, but it is to be inferred that it was part of the South Braintree loot.)

"Their search was fruitless," according to the Globe, "except for finding of an empty RIFLE shell."

Failing to get the fourth shotgun shell into evidence, the commonwealth tried another way to link Vanzetti with the Buick car.

It proceeded to build its case upon the shoulders of two missing men—a shaky scaffolding, but one which served the prosecution's purposes.

It put on the stand Mrs. Simon Johnson, wife of a garage keeper, who at the request of the police, telephoned them when Michael Boda called on the night of May 5 for his own automobile —an Overland— which was stored in the Johnson garage.

She asserted that Sacco and two other Italians were with Boda that night, and was quite certain about it, although her husband testified that Mrs. Johnson was in the light when she observed the four men, and that the visitors were in the shadow. Johnson knew Boda well, and he took an oath that Boda had owned and driven an Overland car, but never to his knowledge had driven a Buick.

Finally, however, the prosecution summoned Napoleon Ensher, a milkman, who said he didn't know Boda by name, but that he knew who was meant, and that he had once seen Boda driving a Buick—maybe four weeks ago, maybe eight weeks ago. There was no showing that Ensher had any knowledge of different makes of automobiles, nor any explanation of how he happened to notice what kind of a car was being driven by a man whose name he didn't know—a man who simply passed one day a long time ago, passed "waving his head." Other makes of automobiles might easily be confused with a Buick by a person unfamiliar with their differences.

On this extremely flimsy evidence, in the face of an alibi that would certainly have been accepted had the defense witnesses been Americans instead of Italians, Vanzetti was convicted of attempted highway robbery and given the enormous sentence of from twelve to fifteen years. The indictment carried two counts: attempt to murder and attempt to rob. Judge Thayer instructed the jury to disregard the first count, but, such was the feeling against the defendant that they brought in a verdict of Guilty on both counts. Sentence however was only passed on the latter. In his charge to the jury Judge Thayer had said that the crime was "cognate with the defendant's ideals" as a radical.

SACCO AND VANZETTI

But what sort of a trap was it into which Sacco and Vanzetti stepped the evening of May 5th?

Their arrest seems to go back to the fact that in the famous January raids Police Chief Stewart of Bridgewater helped Department of Justice agents rout four Lithuanians out of their beds and drag them off to Deer Island. That seems to have started him on a career of red-baiting.

Later, at the request of the Department of Justice, he arrested and engineered the deportation of a certain Coacci, a member of the vaguely outlined group, readers of Galleani's paper, to which Sacco and Vanzetti belonged. Coacci was deported from Ellis Island on April 18, leaving behind a wife who was about to have a baby. Chief Stewart was worrying about the series of holdups, committed it was thought by Italians, which were earning the police considerable adverse criticism in the community. Something had to be done. It was not until Coacci had been shipped off that Stewart got the idea

that perhaps he might be implicated in the Bridgewater and
South Braintree crimes.   It turned out that Coacci had worked
in the L. Q. White shoe factory some time before the Bridgewater
attempt.   Stewart hatched the theory that perhaps the little
house where Coacci lived was the bandit headquarters.   Boda
was a salesman and drove a car.   Stewart found him and
questioned him.   Boda's car was being repaired at Johnson's
garage a little down the road.   Then Stewart found out from
Johnson that the car had been brought in for repairs some time
near the date of the South Braintree murders.   He told him to
phone for the police if anyone came to take Boda's car away.

So Stewart, the small town cop, found himself in charge of
the case.   Captain Proctor, head of the state police, stepped out
after warning him that he thought the trap had snapped on
the wrong birds.   The theory elaborated by him and by Katzmann was that the five men who committed the South Braintree
crime (years later identified by Madeiros as members of the
Morelli gang of Providence) were Boda, Orciani and Coacci,
and after their arrest, Sacco and Vanzetti thrown in to make
up the exact total.   Coacci was escaping with the swag.   Federal
agents had his trunk seized and brought back when he landed
in Italy, but nothing of a suspicious nature was found in it.
Orciani was found to have been at work on the day of the crime.
Boda disappeared.   All of which proved conclusively that Sacco
and Vanzetti were the criminals.

No one who remembers the winter of 1919-20 can deny that
even the mildest radicals, whether citizens or aliens, were looked
upon every man jack of them as criminals and bombers by the
police and good people generally all over the Union.   In
conversation the phrase "He ought to be in jail" followed after
the word Red as naturally as a tail follows a dog.   The news
of the death of Salsedo had thrown the few remaining Italian
radicals round Boston into a panic.   That night Sacco and Vanzetti were trying to hide incriminating literature and at the same
time to call a protest meeting in Brockton on May 9th.   When they
met Boda and Orciani outside the home of the garage-keeper
Johnson in West Bridgewater that night of the fifth, they were
already pretty much alarmed.   When Johnson began to make

excuses to them about Boda's car, saying that they could not take it out as it did not have the proper license plate, they must have felt pretty uneasy. Actually Mrs. Johnson was telephoning the police. Boda's car was a small Overland, that would have been hard to match with the Buick that was being looked for in connection with the South Braintree crime, but the $2,000 reward offered by the shoe factory was worth taking a chance for. Probably the very fact of four wops wanting to go riding in a car was suspicious to the Johnsons. Anyway the four men got nervous. Boda and Orciani rode off on Orciani's motorcycle, and Sacco and Vanzetti got aboard a street car. Crossing into Brockton they were arrested. The police though they were arresting Boda.

We're going to be deported, thought Sacco and Vanzetti, and naturally did their best not to implicate their friends and comrades.

The fact that they were armed was a piece of horrible bad luck. If it hadn't been for the revolvers and shotgun shells found on them they would probably have been released as was Orciani whom the police picked up a couple of days later. But why were they armed, everybody asks. Vanzetti had bought the gun to protect his earnings as a fish-peddler. It was a time of many holdups. Sacco was accustomed to carry a gun as night watchman at the Three K's Factory. A great many people of all classes get a feeling of strength and manhood out of toting a gun. Put yourself in their place. Haven't there been times when you who are reading this would have been pretty embarrassed to explain your actions if suddenly arrested and bullied and crossquestioned by a lot of bulls in a station house? Add to that the chance connection of revolvers, shells, the draft of an anarchist leaflet. Many a man has died in the Chair on flimsier evidence than that. That's always the answer of the man in the street when you press him about this case. Many a good guy's been electrocuted on less than that.

It's time that you realized fully, you who are reading this, man or woman, laborer or whitecollar worker, that if Sacco and Vanzetti die in the Chair as the result of a frameup based on an unlucky accident, your chance of life will be that much slimmer, if you ever come to be arrested as a result of a similar unlucky chain of circumstances. Justice can't be embalmed in the dome of a courthouse. It's got to be worked for, fought for daily by those who want it for themselves and for their neighbors.

A great many men and women do realize it. That's why Sacco and Vanzetti are alive today.

So it was that it was as a convicted highway robber that Vanzetti was tried for murder with Sacco. If it hadn't been for that fact it would have been much harder to convict the two men at Dedham.

By one of those agreements of counsel that seem so ghastly to a layman, the defense contracted not to produce character witnesses for Vanzetti, if the prosecution abstained from bringing up the previous conviction. It was a skeleton in the closet, never mentioned, but on everyone's mind all through the trial.

X

THE DEDHAM TRIAL

Sacco and Vanzetti were found guilty of committing a $15,776 payroll robbery and murdering Frederick Parmenter, paymaster, and Alexander Berardelli, payroll guard, at South Braintree, Mass., on April 15, 1920. Parmenter and Berardelli were employees of the Slater and Morrill Shoe Company.

Both defendants were tried before Superior Judge Webster Thayer at Dedham in June and July 1921, the trial extending seven weeks, and were convicted of first degree murder by a jury which the defense attorneys contend was irregularly and illegally selected. The verdict carries a penalty of death in the electric chair.

The crime was committed at 3.05 p. m. on Pearl street, in front of the four-story Rice and Hutchins shoe factory. This building was filled with workers. Four rows of windows looked out upon the scene of the shooting. While the glass in them was opaque, as soon as the shots were heard, many windows were thrown open.

Many other workers saw the crime from the windows of the Slater and Morrill shoe factory a short distance west of the Rice and Hutchins plant. And directly opposite was an excavation where numerous laborers were at work.

Just before the shooting a train had come in letting off passengers at the nearby railroad station. Numerous persons were on the street as the bandits fled, their number swelled quickly by the sound of the shots and the wave of excitement that traveled like the wind through the small town. Westward on Pearl Street the bandit-automobile sped, crossing the New Haven tracks increasing in speed as it proceeded, and continuing the main streets of the town.

This was but one of a series of payroll robberies in Eastern Massachusetts, of which the perpetrators had invariably escaped. These bandits too, got away. The authorities were on the defensive; public indignation was high. Search for the bandits was participated in by the state police and local police, with the active co-operation of the Department of Justice and various agencies employed by the allied manufacturing and banking interests. These included the Pinkerton Detective Agency, acting in the behalf of the Travelers' Insurance Company, which insured the Slater and Morrill payroll. Investigation by these forces continued from April 15, 1920 to May 31, 1921, when Sacco and Vanzetti were brought to trial.

Of the scores who saw the crime and escape, and with so many powerful agencies co-operating in the search, how many witnesses were brought against Sacco and Vanzetti? A trifling number, as will appear in this analysis; while a very much larger number of those who saw the crime are positive that neither Sacco nor Vanzetti were the bandits.

Several important witnesses for the prosecution were seriously discredited, while various responsible persons who saw the events connected with the crime and who declared that the arrested men were not the bandits, were pushed aside by the state after it interviewed them.

Here follows a careful analysis of the actual testimony for Sacco and Vanzetti. This analysis is the result of a searching study of the 3,900 pages of official transcript. Every statement set down here, unless otherwise specified, is borne out by the court record.

The mass of evidence which went toward the setting of the crime but which had no bearing on the guilt or innocence of the accused is eliminated, while evidence introduced piecemeal and in haphazard order is assembled and arranged under appropriate heads.

The testimony relating only to Vanzetti is presented first because it is the shorter and thus more easily disentangled from the mass of detail under which its inadequacy was hidden. Such an arrangement throws into bold relief the injustice of the court's refusal to separate the trials of the two men. A request for the separation was entered by the defense at the opening and again at the close of the trial. "Where is there anything prejudicial to Vanzetti," asked the judge, "if proper instructions are given to the jury?" But juries, despite formal instruction to count this fact against Defendant No. 1 and that fact against Defendant No. 2, inevitably tend to count all facts against both when they are tried together. The human mind is not a mechanical instrument which functions according to judicial instructions.

Then the case against Sacco is treated in full, and finally the evidence applicable to both men is analyzed.

TESTIMONY RELATING ONLY TO VANZETTI

In weighing the testimony against Vanzetti, it should be borne in mind that the prosecution admitted it had no evidence that Vanzetti took any part in the shooting. He was never given a preliminary examination on the South Braintree crime and did not know on what ground he would be linked with that crime until he heard it at the trial.

The prosecution sought to connect him with the murder by producing one witness—solitary, uncorroborated and conceded by the prosecution to be "mistaken" in one part of his observations—who claimed fourteen months after the event, to "identify" Vanzetti as among the bandits; two detached witnesses who claimed to have seen him on the morning of the crime in or near

Braintree; one other who claims to have seen him in the bandit-car some miles distant after the crime; one witness who claimed to have seen him in a trolley car in another town on the evening before or following the crime, and by an attempt to show that a revolver found in Vanzetti's possession belonged to Berardelli, one of the men murdered, but this fizzled completely.

The defense countered by introducing impeaching evidence of all the so-called "identifications" and by bringing strong alibi witnesses.

Of the score of witnesses for both sides who described some portion of the murder scene, 35 claimed to have gotten a sufficiently good view to describe the face of one or more of the bandits. The only one of these who identified Vanzetti was Michael Levangie, gate tender for the N. Y., N. H. & H. railroad at South Braintree. This man was in his shanty on the west side of the tracks when the shooting occurred. He had lowered the gates for an oncoming train; then he saw an automobile coming from the east.

In that car sitting beside the driver, Levangie said, a man waved a revolver at him, motioning him to raise the gates, and the car sped across. The man with the pistol snapped the trigger at the gateman as the automobile passed. Levangie declared the driver was dark complexioned, with black hair, heavy brown moustache, cheek-bones sticking out, slouch hat, army coat. He identified the driver as Vanzetti.

The District Attorney in his closing argument admitted that Vanzetti could not have been at the wheel, as the testimony was overwhelming that the driver was a light, consumptive looking man. The defense brought four witnesses who absolutely impeached Levangie's assertions in toto:

Henry McCarthy, fireman on the New Haven, talked with Levangie a few minutes after the shooting. Levangie told him he didn't get a look at the bandits, and was so scared he ran for cover. McCarthy volunteered to testify for the defense after reading Levangie's assertions in the newspapers.

Edward Carter, shoe-worker for Slater and Morrill, testified that Levangie told him at 4:15 P. M. that day, the driver was light-complexioned.

Alexander Victorson, a freight clerk at South Braintree, heard Levangie say immediately after the shooting, "it would be hard to identify those men."

John L. Sullivan, gate tender who takes shifts with Levangie, was told by Levangie, about two weeks before the trial that he had been interviewed by J. J. McAnarney, counsel for the defense, and that he had told him he was unable to identify anyone. Under cross-examination, Levangie first acknowledged that he remembered this interview. Later he declared, "I don't remember anything about it," and denied having ever told anyone that he was unable to identify the bandits. Asked if he had ever described the driver as a "light complexioned, Swedish or Norwegian type of person," he answered, "No, sir."

Levangie was a loose-jointed fellow, with a shifty eye and a look of cunning in his face. He appeared wholly unabashed at the contradictions brought out during his cross-examination. Rather he had the manner of regarding the whole proceedings as a joke. It would be difficult to imagine a witness less entitled to carry weight. Yet his "identification" was the sole evidence of Vanzetti's presence at the murder scene.

The other identification witnesses of Vanzetti referred to times and places other than those of the crime. They were Faulkner, Dolbeare, Reed, and by a stretch of liberality also Cole.

John W. Fulkner averred that he left Cohasset on the 9:23 a. m. train on April 15. At three stations he was asked by a man across the aisle if this was East Braintree. The inquirer said that a man behind him wanted to know. Faulkner identified Vanzetti as the man in back. This man alighted at East Braintree.

The improbability that any man on his way to commit murder should attract attention to himself and to the point at which he was to meet his companions in crime, is heightened if applied to Vanzetti who is a man of superior intelligence and who had made frequent journeys on that railroad line.

The morning after the murder, when the news of the crime was published, it occurred to Faulkner that perhaps the Italian on the train might be mixed up with the affair. Then came the arrest and the publication of Sacco's and Vanzetti's pictures. But Faulkner, with the episode fresh in his mind, did nothing. Two months later he was taken to make an identification. At Dedham he testified positively, "He is the man," indicating Vanzetti in the cage opposite to him.

At one point defense counsel McAnarney suddenly requested a certain man in the audience to step forward, a dark man with a big moustache like Vanzetti's, and Faulkner was asked:

"Isn't this the man you saw on the train?"

"I don't know. He might be."

But the dark man bore little resemblance to Vanzetti, except for the big moustache. His name, Joseph Scavitto.

In contradiction of Faulkner's claim, the defense put on the stand the conductor of the train, who certified that no ticket had been collected from Plymouth to East Braintree or to Braintree on that day, and that no cash fare had been paid; and it put on the stand the ticket agents of Plymouth, of Seaside, first station out of Plymouth, and Kingston, the second station out of Plymouth, all of whom testified that no ticket had been sold to either of the above points.

While the jury was being drawn, Harry Dolbeare, piano tuner from South Braintree, was excused from service after a whispered conversation with the judge. Summoned later as a prosecution witness, he testified that he asked to be excused because he recognized Vanzetti in court as a man he saw in South Braintree on April 15, *fourteen months before he testified.*

Dolbeare asserted that on that uneventful morning he saw an automobile moving along the street with five men in it, and he noticed particularly the middle man of the three in the rear seat. This man was leaning forward talking with somebody in the front. Dolbeare got only a profile view of him against the background of the black curtain.

"What was it about them that attracted your attention?" asked Attorney McAnarney.

"The appearance of the whole five attracted me. They were strangers to me, and appeared to be foreigners."

"What else?"

"Well, that carload was a tough-looking bunch."

Dolbeare agreed that he had seen many cars containing three, five or seven foreigners coming from the Fore River shipyards.

"Give me some description of the men on the front seat," said McAnarney.

"I wouldn't like to be on record, for my impression isn't firm enough. The men on the front seat impressed me hardly any."

He thought they wore old clothes, but he didn't know whether they wore overalls and jumpers, nor whether they were clean or grimy.

"Give me some description of the other men on the back seat," demanded McAnarney.

But Dolbeare couldn't give a single detail except that they were a "tough-looking bunch." All the excitement attendant upon the murders in Braintree that day didn't impel him to inform the authorities that he had seen a tough-looking bunch in an automobile, nor did he go to Brockton police station with the big delegation which went from Braintree after Sacco and Vanzetti were arrested. Even the photographs of Vanzetti published broadcast then did not move him to any action.

At 4:15 P. M. on the crime-date, Austin T. Reed, gate-tender at the Matfield Crossing, some miles distant from South Braintree put the gates down for a passing train and brought a big touring car to a stand. "A dark complexioned man" with "kind of hollow cheeks, high cheek bones—stubbed moustache" wearing a slouch hat, called out in "clear and unmistakable" English, "What in hell are you holding us up for?"

Three weeks later, when Sacco and Vanzetti had been arrested and many persons were being taken to the Brockton jail to look them over, Reed went to Brockton, "looked for an Italian," as he testified under cross examination, an Italian with a moustache, and Vanzetti filled the bill. He recognized not only the appearance, but the voice, which speaking in the jail in a conversational tone and in Italian, recalled to the witness "that same gruff voice" in which the Italian had hollered at him from the automobile. This witness was certain of his "identification," although Vanzetti's moustache is the opposite of "stubbed" and his accent is noticeably foreign.

It is to be noted that Reed placed the moustached man with whom he "identified" Vanzetti, on the front seat beside the driver, the location in which almost every other witness had placed the bandit with whom it was sought to identify Sacco.

One other witness, Austin C. Cole, conductor on the trolley car into Brockton on which Sacco and Vanzetti were arrested on the evening of May 5th following the crime, testified that these same men had ridden on his car at the same hour on either April 14th or 15th. If this testimony is accepted as to the 14th, it discredits Faulkner's testimony as to the passenger on the train from Cohasset the following morning. And if it is accepted as to the 15th, then it claims that two red-handed murderers, one of whom had been in the lime-light before scores of spectators, left their high power automobile to board a trolley several hours later in a town not far from the scene of their crime.

Under cross examination Cole admitted that when the two men boarded the car in April he thought at first the larger man was "Tony the Portuguese," whom he had known in Campello for a dozen years.

Defense Counsel McAnarney showed Cole a profile photograph of a man with a large dark moustache.

Q. Do you recognize that picture?

A. It looks like Vanzetti. (Cole, of course was sitting where he could see Vanzetti plainly as he answered.)

Q. That is a picture of Vanzetti?

A. That is what I would call it.

Q. And not a picture of your friend Tony? A. No.

At this juncture a man was brought into the courtroom.

Q. Do you know this man? A. I have met him, yes.

Q. Who is he? A. Tony.

McAnarney showed the picture to Cole again.

Q. Is that a picture of Vanzetti?

A. It looks like it.

But actually it was a photograph of another Italian, wholly unlike Vanzetti except that he has a big moustache.

The foregoing is the whole case against Vanzetti in the way of identification.

It was the theory of the government that the Harrison & Richardson revolver which Vanzetti carried when arrested had been taken from Berardelli's dead body by the bandit who shot him. No one had seen this done. Prosecutor Katzmann based the theory on evidence that Berardelli was known to have carried a revolver (whether of similar make is unknown), which had been seen in Berardelli's possession and handled by a prosecution witness, James F. Bostock, the Saturday previous to the shooting, and that no weapon was found on Berardelli after his death.

Three weeks before the murders, however, Berardelli took his revolver to the Iver Johnson Company in Boston for repairs, according to testimony given by his widow, Mrs. Sarah Berardelli. She accompanied him on the trip. The gun had a broken spring.

Berardelli had obtained the revolver originally from his superior, Parmenter, and he gave the repair check to Parmenter so that the latter could take the gun out after it was repaired, the widow stated. "I don't know whether the revolver ever came back... Mr. Parmenter let him have another revolver, with a black handle like the first."

Mrs. Berardelli did not identify the Vanzetti revolver as her husband's.

Lincoln Wadsworth, in charge of gun repairing at the Iver Johnson Company, testified that the company's records show that Berardelli brought in a 38-calibre Harrington and Richardson revolver for repairs on March 20. But Geo. Fitzmeyer, gunsmith for that firm, testified that a revolver on Repair Job No. 94765 was a 32-calibre gun. The company's records, according to the testimony of James H. Jones, manager of the firearms department, do not show whether the revolver repaired on Job No. 94765 was ever delivered.

When Fitzmeyer was testifying, he was asked to examine the Vanzetti pistol, and he declared that a new hammer had recently been put into that gun. But he found no indications that any new spring had lately been put into it.

Of important, almost conclusive, bearing upon the state theory is the testimony of Mrs. Aldeah Florence, the friend with whom Mrs. Berardelli made her home after her husband's death. She testified that the day following the funeral, while in conversation with the widow she had lamented "Oh, dear, if he had taken my advice and taken the revolver out of the shop, maybe he wouldn't be in the same condition he is today." The government might have called Mrs. Berardelli to the witness stand to contradict this evidence had it believed it to be untrue, but did not do so. If Mrs. Florence's testimony stands, and the government did not challenge it, then the rest of the voluminous testimony relative to the pistol is irrelevant.

Vanzetti's gun was traced from owner to owner until no doubt remained as to its identity.

If the evidence against Vanzetti was slight, there was nevertheless the fact, never referred to, but in everybody's mind, which cannot fail to have been counted as evidence, that upon his arrest he had been at first charged, not with complicity in the South Braintree crime, but as principal in the attempted holdup at Bridgewater.

Under the forms of legal procedure, there was no chance to put in the plea that the earlier trial for the Bridgewater crime was believed by those who had studied the transcript of evidence to have been an almost grotesque travesty of justice. The Bridgewater crime stalked behind and overshadowed all the evidence introduced against Vanzetti at Dedham.

The failure on the part of Judge Webster Thayer to separate the two trials made it inevitable that this shadow (and no amount of instructions could remove it) also covered Sacco.

Bartolomeo Vanzetti declared on the witness stand that he was in Plymouth, 35 miles from South Braintree all day on April 15. He gave names of persons to whom he sold fish; told of buying a piece of suiting from Joseph Rosen, a woolen peddler; and of talking with Melvin Corl, a fisherman, while Corl was painting a boat by the sea.

Vanzetti's alibi was supported by eleven undiscredited witnesses.

Mrs. Alphonsine Brini testified that Vanzetti brought fish

to her home in Cherry Court, Plymouth, about 10 a. m. April 15. He came back about noon with Rosen, and asked her to examine and pass upon the quality of cloth he had bought for a suit. Mrs. Brini fixed the date by the fact that she had been home a week from the hospital, and that her husband telephoned that day to Dr. Shurtleff for a nurse.

Miss Lefevre Brini, 15, stated that Vanzetti delivered fish at the Brini home about 10 o'clock on April 15. She had remained home from work that day to care for her mother, who was ill.

Miss Gertrude Mathews, nurse in medical department of Plymouth Cordage Company, recalled telephone conversation with Dr. Shurtleff regarding the matter of attending Mrs. Brini. Was at Brini home to attend her from April 15 to April 20, inclusive.

Mrs. Ella Urquhart, another nurse at the cordage plant, recalled the same message from Dr. Shurtleff.

Joseph Rosen, woolen peddler, testified that he met Vanzetti in Suosso's Lane, Plymouth, shortly before noon on April 15. Vanzetti was pushing his fish-cart. They were acquainted. Rosen had sold him cloth before. Sold him a piece of suiting now with a hole in it, "at a bargain"; went with Vanzetti to Brini home to show goods to Mrs. Brini.

Several other persons in Plymouth bought cloth from him that day, Rosen averred. Rosen was actually one of the strongest witnesses in Vanzetti's defense. The prosecution never attempted to disprove his story of his presence in Plymouth on the day of the crime. If that story had not been true, it would have been easy for the commonwealth to have discredited Rosen by producing the various persons to whom he said he made sales. One of these was the wife of the police chief of Plymouth.

But the prosecution did not produce any of these persons as witnesses, and Rosen's story stands unshaken in every detail.

That evening Rosen went by train to Whitman, a small town near Brockton. There he read in the Brockton papers about the payroll murders at South Braintree, and he heard many people there talking about the crime. He stayed that night at a small hotel in Whitman. Next day he returned to Boston.

Three weeks later he read of the arrest of Sacco and Vanzetti. Remembering Vanzetti well, he fixed the date by his memory that when he had reached Whitman, all the town was talking about the South Braintree murders.

He also fixed that date as April 15 with reference to a receipt for taxes, paid by his wife on that date, and about which he had spoken to her before leaving home. The receipt was produced in court.

Miss Lillian Schuler, waitress in hotel at Whitman, testified that she rented a room to a man on the night of April 15. Register simply shows that a man occupied the room, and gives no name.

Melvin Corl, Plymouth fisherman, testified that he was painting a boat on the afternoon of April 15. Vanzetti came down to the shore and talked with him for an hour. Corl fixed the date by reference to his wife's birthday which fell on April 17th, on which date he launched the boat and made a trip to Duxbury to tow a boat back, for which he received $5.00.

Angelo Giadobone of Plymouth bought fish of Vanzetti on April 15. Remembered date with relation to April 19, when he was operated on for appedicitis. Giadobone said he still owed Vanzetti for the fish.

Antonio Carbone of Plymouth attested that he sold fish to Vanzetti on April 15.

TESTIMONY RELATING ONLY TO SACCO

The government sought to establish Sacco as the dark man "needing a shave" who leaned against the fence below the Rice & Hutchins factory, shot Berardelli, jumped into the automobile and leaning out shot right and left as the car fled through the town. Towards that end, it brought into court four alleged eyewitnesses of the crime and escape who "identified" Sacco. These four were Miss Splaine, Miss Devlin, Pelser and Goodridge. Two others called for the same purpose, Wade and De Berardinis, disappointed the prosecution by their failure to identify.

Mary Eva Splaine, bookkeper for Slater and Morrill, gave a remarkably complete description of one of the bandits in the fleeing car, considering that she was in a second-story window a minimum distance of 80 feet from the car, and saw the bandit only in the brief time required for an automobile to travel 35 feet at 18 miles an hour—which is one and one-fifth seconds. She saw the car first from an east window; then switched to a window facing south. As she stepped to the south window, a man leaned out from behind the front seat.

"He was slightly taller than I," she testified; "weighed about 140 to 145 pounds, had dark hair, dark eyebrows, thin cheeks, and clean-shaven face of a peculiar greenish-white. His forehead was high. His hair was brushed back, and it was, I should think, between two and two and a half inches long. His shoulders were straight out, square. He wore no hat... His face was clear-cut, clean-cut. He wore a gray shirt. He was a muscular, active looking man, and had a strong left hand, a powerful hand."

She said he was leaning half out of the car, just behind the front seat, and that his left hand was on the back of that seat, presumably at arm's length from his face.

"He was in my view from the middle of the distance between the railroad tracks and the cobbler shop, a distance probably 60 to 70 feet, and half distance would be 30 to 35 feet. My view was cut off by the cobbler shop."

Miss Splaine declared positively that Sacco was the bandit who leaned from the car. Defense Counsel Fred H. Moore confronted her with the record of the preliminary hearing in the Sacco case, which shows that at that time, a year before the trial and a few weeks after the crime and after she had looked Sacco over to her complete satisfaction on three different days, she admitted under oath that she "could not swear positively that Sacco was the bandit."

"That is not true," she now asserted. "I never said it."

But next day she came into court and announced that she wished to change her testimony, and admitted she had said at the preliminary hearing that she could not swear positively Sacco was the bandit. (Page 416, official transcript.) She added that her present certainty of Sacco's being the bandit came from "reflection." The transcript of the preliminary testimony (Page 56) showed that she had said in police court: "I do not think my opportunity afforded me the right to say he is the man."

In the preliminary hearing she remembered a revolver in the right hand. At the trial she recalled nothing about the right hand or this revolver.

Finally she admitted that when she visited state police headquarters in Boston shortly after the crime, she was shown a rogues' gallery photograph of a certain man. Of him she said: "He bears a striking resemblance to the bandit."

Later she learned that this man was in Sing Sing prison on April 15.

Frances J. Devlin, also a bookkeeper for Slater and Morrill, gave testimony similar to that of Miss Splaine. She saw the escaping car from the same observation point, a window in the second story of the Hampton House, at least 80 feet from the car. She said she saw a man in the right rear seat of the automobile lean out and fire at the crowd.

This bandit, she said, was fairly thick-set, dark, pale, rather good looking, with clear features. His hair grew away from his temples, and was blown back. She "positively identified" Sacco as the bandit.

Under cross examination Miss Devlin admitted she had testified in the preliminary hearing that the bandit was tall and well-built, while Sacco is only 5 feet 6 inches tall. She admitted she said then: "I don't say positively he is the man."

The Quincy police court record shows she said at the preliminary hearing that she got a better view of the chauffeur's face than of the other bandit's. This was manifestly impossible as the car was covered and had a left-hand drive. But at the trial she declared that she never said that; and now said that she did not see the chauffeur's face.

She admitted that Sacco was made to assume postures like that of the bandit for her in Brockton police station.

Answering questions by Prosecutor Harold Williams, Miss Devlin explained she had testified in the lower court that she couldn't say positively that Sacco was the bandit "because of the immensity of the crime. I felt sure in my own mind, but I hated to say so, out and out."

In spite of the seemingly impossible detail of the descriptions of these two young women, considering their position and the extreme brevity of the period of observation, in spite of the manner in which doubt at the preliminary hearings changed into certainty in the final trial, they were the strongest witnesses against Sacco.

The third of these witnesses, Louis Pelser, went to pieces on the stand. He was a shoe-cutter in the Rice and Hutchins factory, working on the first floor above the raised basement. Pelser asserted that through the crack of an opened window he saw a man sinking on the pavement, that he opened a window, and that he stood up amid flying bullets and did two things— he wrote down the number of the approaching bandit-automobile and he made a mental note of one bandit who was shooting at the fallen Berardelli. This witness declared that he noticed even the pin in the bandit's collar.

"I wouldn't say it was him," Pleser said, "but Sacco is a dead image of him."

Then Pelser proceeded to tangle himself up in lie after lie. He admitted he had lied to Robert Reid, defense investigator, "to avoid being a witness," and that he had told Reid he didn't see anything because he got scared and ducked under a bench. Next he denied ever discussing the case with any one previous to Reid's interview with him, but later admitted he had talked with a state detective previous to that time.

Cross examination revealed that Pelser had been out of work for some time after the tragedy, and had been re-employed by Rice and Hutchins two months before the trial. Subsequently he told his foreman he had testimony to give. On the morning of the day Pelser appeared in court, he talked with Prosecutor Williams, was shown Sacco's picture and was taken to identify him. Fourteen months had elapsed between the crime-date and the day on which Pelser purported to identify Sacco on the witness-stand at Dedham.

Pelser was noticeably embarrassed on the stand, mopping his forehead continually, shifting his weight from foot to foot, and unable to understand the simplest questions. Further his testimony was contradicted by three fellow-workers:

William Brenner declared it was he and not Pelser whose station was near the partly open window, and that it was McCollum who opened the window fully. He said that McCollum shouted: "They are shooting; duck!" and that they all dropped down behind the bench. When the shots sounded farther away, they got up again, looked out, somebody got the automobile number and wrote it on the work-bench. By that time the car was near the railroad tracks.

Peter McCollum declared that it was he and not Pelser who threw open the window and shut it again instantly, then dropped down behind the work-bench with his fellows. He was the only one who looked out of the open window during the shooting, he swore. Opaque glass was in all the windows in the work room.

Dominic Costantino confirmed Brenner's and McCollum's testimony. He saw Pelser get under the bench along with the rest. He heard him say afterward that he didn't see anyone. He volunteered as a witness after reading Pelser's testimony in the Globe.

The last of the crime-scene witnesses against Sacco, Carlos E. Goodridge, is a phonograph salesman. He testified that he was in a poolroom on Pearl street a few doors west of the Hampton House. He heard shots, stepped out, saw the bandit-automobile coming; when it was 20 or 25 feet away a man pointed a gun at him; he went back into the poolroom. Man with gun was dark, smooth-shaven, bareheaded, pointed face, dark suit. Goodridge identified Sacco as that man.

Four witnesses including the proprietor of the poolroom gave the lie to this witness:

Peter Magazu, the poolroom proprietor, declared that when Goodridge came back into the poolroom he said the bandit he saw was light-haired; and he had said: "This job wasn't pulled by any foreign people."

Harry Arrigoni, barber, related that Goodridge said a week after the shooting that he couldn't identify any of the bandits.

Nicola D'Amato, another barber, said Goodridge told him on

April 15 he was in the poolroom when the bandit-car passed and did not see anybody in the automobile.

Andrew Mangano, music store owner and former employer of Goodridge, testified that he had urged him to go to see if he could identify the suspects in jail, and that Goodridge told him it was useless; he couldn't identify the bandits. Mangano declared that Goodridge's reputation for truth and veracity was bad.

With the jury absent, the defense endeavored to introduce testimony to show that when Goodridge first identified Sacco in September, 1920, (when Vanzetti was in this same courtroom in Dedham for a hearing), Goodridge was in court to answer a charge of absconding with funds belonging to his employer. Judge Thayer barred that evidence on the ground that no final judgment was entered in the Goodridge case. Goodridge simply pleaded guilty to the theft, and the case was "filed."

Lewis L. Wade was a disappointment to the prosecution, as he was one of those upon whose testimony the indictment of Sacco was based. He was an employee of Slater and Morrill, and was in the street when the crime occurred, saw Berardelli shot from a distance of 72 paces. Just then a car came up; the man at the wheel was pale, 30 to 35 years old, looked sick. The assailant threw a cash box into the car and jumped in.

This man was described by Wade as short, bareheaded, 26 or 27, weighed about 140, hair blown back, needed shave, hair cut with "feather edge" in back. Wore gray shirt.

"Have you seen the man who shot Berardelli since?" asked Prosecutor Williams.

"I thought I saw him in Brockton police station," Wade answered. "I thought then it was Sacco."

But Wade declared now that he wasn't sure. He had felt "a little mite of doubt" when he had testified in the preliminary hearing at Quincy. "I might be mistaken," he had then testified. His doubt deepened about four weeks before he took the witness stand. "I was in a barber shop, and a man came in. His face looked familiar. The more I looked at that man and the more I thought about him the more I thought he resembled the man who killed Berardelli."

Another heavy setback awaited the prosecution in the testimony of Louis De Berardinis, cobbler, who it was claimed had "identified" at Brockton. His shop is on Pearl Street with the Hampton building behind, a grass plot being between. He heard shots, ran out of shop, saw bandit-car coming across tracks, man jumping in. Man leaned out of the car with gun in hand, came opposite, pointed gun at him, pulled trigger; no explosion.

"That bandit was pale, had a long face, awful white," said De Berardinis, "and he had light hair. A thin fellow, light weight. Not like Sacco. The one I saw was light. Sacco is dark."

This is the complete identification case against Sacco so far as the murder scene is concerned. As has been shown, Pelser is discredited by his self-contradictions on the stand, and both his testimony and Goodridge's is refuted by several undiscredited witnesses. The two bookkeepers were at a disadvantage in their location for purposes of identification, and they were positive fourteen months after the crime, whereas only a few weeks after it, they had expressed some uncertainty.

In addition to the above six, the government put five witnesses on the stand who got a sufficiently good view of bandit with whom it was sought to identify Sacco to describe his appearance; namely, Carrigan, Bostock, McGlone, Langlois, and Behrsin. None of them were able to make an identification. It is of prime importance that their location were such as to make their testimony applicable to the same bandit whom the four "positive witnesses" identify as Sacco.

Mark E. Carrigan, shoe-worker employed by Slater and Morrill on the third floor of the Hampton House related that he saw Parmenter and Berardelli proceeding from the offices to the main factory with the payroll money, and that he presently heard shooting and saw the bandit-automobile coming east on Pearl street past the Hampton House. He saw a dark Italian-looking man in the car with a revolver.

But he could not identify either defendant as being in that car. Carrigan's testimony has a large bearing upon the credibility of Miss Splaine and Miss Devlin, who from a window one floor below where Carrigan was, claimed to identify Sacco as a

man who was leaning out of the escaping automobile. Eight
feet below Carrigan, the two women were no more than a foot
closer to the bandits than he.

James F. Bostock, machine installer of Brockton, had been
doing work for Slater and Morrill. Shortly before the shooting,
he came out of the Slater factory and walked west on Pearl
street. He passed two men, who were leaning against a fence
arguing. It is not disputed that one of these was the man who
shot Berardelli.

Immediately afterward he meet Parmenter and Berardelli
coming down the road with the payroll boxes. Bostock was a
close friend of Parmenter. They exchanged words in a momentary meeting. Just after Bostock had left the paymaster, he
heard shots, turned, and saw Parmenter and Berardelli fall.
The men he had seen at the fence were shooting. They grabbed
the money-boxes and jumped into an oncoming automobile.

Bostock ran around the corner of a high board fence along
the New Haven track. The bandit-car passed so close, he said,
that he could have touched it with his hand.

He said he could not identify either of the defendants as the
highwaymen.

James E. McGlone, teamster, helped lower Parmenter to the
ground after the fatal shot. McGlone had been working in the
excavation. When the shooting started he ran forward, and saw
the bandits at close range. The commonwealth didn't ask him
if he could identify. Defendants' counsel had not interviewed
him. They asked him in court if he could identify the defendants,
and he said he could not.

Edgar C. Langlois, foreman of Rice and Hutchins, was on
the second floor (from the street level) of that factory, facing
on the crime-scene. He could make no identification. The only
description he could give was that the highwaymen he saw were
"stout, thick-chested—that is, full-chested," a description which
fits neither Sacco nor Vanzetti.

Langlois' testimony is highly significant because he was in
a central window immediately above the window from which
another prosecution witness, Pelser, claimed he observed Sacco.
This witness occupies a responsible position in Rice and Hutchins.

Hans Behrsin, chauffeur for Mr. Slater of the robbed shoe company, testified for the prosecution. He was sitting in a stationary sedan on the right-hand side of Pearl street, a little beyond the poolroom.

Five men were in the automobile, Behrsin said. They passed him within ten feet. One man was leaning out. The car was going 16 to 18 miles an hour. He could not identify either defendant as being one of the bandits. A few moments earlier he had noticed the two bandits just before they opened fire, and he described them as light-complexioned.

The government contends further that the bandits had lingered about South Braintree during the morning. Precisely as against Vanzetti, three witnesses uncorroborated—unless impeachment be an inverted kind of corroboration—were brought forward in support of the contention that Sacco had been seen in the town that morning.

William S. Tracy, elderly real estate dealer, testified that about 11:45 he saw two men leaning against the window of a drugstore building he owned. They were "clean-shaven, smooth-faced, respectably dressed." He entered the drug store, came out, and drove away in his automobile. Returning a few minutes later, he found the men still there, talking. Again he went away and again he came back, and they still were propped against the window.

Tracy identified Sacco as one of these men: "I would not be positive," he said, "but to the best of my recollection he is the same man."

His statement that the two men were "respectably dressed" contrasts with that of various prosecution witnesses who swore the bandits were rough-looking and needed a shave.

In cross-examination it developed that in February, 1921, Tracy was taken to the Dedham jail and escorted through various departments, and was shown large groups of prisoners, and that finally he was taken over to "the pit," where Sacco was all alone; then he made his "identification."

Tracy's testimony is open to wide question. He stands out in stark isolation from the scores or even hundreds of persons who must have stood upon or passed that corner in that noon-hour, for it is the principal intersection of South Braintree, where innumerable people wait daily for electric cars.

Consider, too, that this corner is only a few hundred feet from the scene of the crime, that Sacco had worked at Rice and Hutchins', and was known presumably by sight to various workers in South Braintree. The defense argues that it is unreasonable to suppose that Sacco, had he been intending to commit robbery and wanton murder in that town within three hours would have lingered on that corner.

William J. Heron, railroad police officer, testified that he saw two men in the New Haven station at South Braintree on April 15. One was 5 feet 6, the other 5 feet 11. He identified Sacco as the smaller man. He noticed the two men he said, "because they acted nervous and... they were smoking cigarettes, one of them." (Page 884, official transcript.)

Q. Which one was smoking? A. The tallest one.

Q. Did you pay much attention to the men when you first came in? A. Not much, only I saw them smoking.

Heron, too, said that the man he saw wore a hat and was respectably dressed, which conflicts with descriptions of the murderer.

Neither man had any outstanding physical characteristics, according to Heron. He admitted he didn't see Sacco to identify him until six weeks later.

After Police Chief Stewart of Bridgewater and State Policeman Brouillard had lined up Heron as a witness for the prosecution, the defense sent an investigator, Robert Reid, to interrogate Heron. He refused to give the defense any information. When asked in cross-examination why he refused to talk to Reid he gave a curious answer for a man who had been a police officer six years.

"Because I didn't want to be brought into it."

This man's testimony was attacked by the defense from the same angle that Tracy's story was attacked. Defense counsel asked: Is it reasonable to suppose that Sacco, if intending to rob and kill three hours later in that town where he had worked, would have lingered in places where many persons would have opportunity to observe him?

Mrs. Lola Andrews, a lady of miscellaneous avocations, attested that on the morning of the crime-date she and Mrs. Julia Campbell went from Quincy to South Braintree to seek work in the shoe factories. They arrived between 11.00 and 11:30. Mrs. Andrews said that she saw an automobile in front of the Slater and Morrill plant, and a man working around the hood.

When they came out of the Slater factory, this man was under the car fixing something. She called him from beneath the car, she asserted, and asked him how to get into the Rice and Hutchins' factory. She identified this man as Sacco.

But at that moment, according to her own statements, another man was standing near that automobile—a light-complexioned emaciated Swedish-looking man. Mrs. Andrews' testimony does not explain why she addressed her inquiry to the man under the automobile instead of asking the man standing near.

While Mrs. Andrews was being cross-examined by Defense Attorney Moore, and when he was showing her some photographs she fainted, and was carried out. Prosecutor Katzmann left the room, returned, scanned the faces of the audience, then conferred in whispers with the court. Judge Thayer ordered the courtroom doors closed, and various spectators were searched.

When the witness took the stand again, she asserted that she fainted because she saw a man in court whom she thought was the person who assaulted her in February, 1920, in a toilet in the Quincy lodging house where she had rooms.

Her testimony was impeached by five defense witnesses. The most important of these was Mrs. Julia Campbell, who accompanied Mrs. Andrews to South Braintree that day, and gave testimony directly opposite.

An elderly but active woman, Mrs. Campbell had come from Maine to testify for the defense after a state detective had told her she needn't go to Massachusetts to testify; that she didn't know anything of importance; and that it would cost too much to have her make the trip.

She submitted to an eyesight test in court at the hands of District Attorney Katzmann, and proved that she was able to distinguish objects and colors at long distance; one instance was her specifying the color of a hat picked at random among the audience. And she had been working in the shoe factories as a stitcher, at a task which requires unerring vision.

"Neither of us spoke to the man under the automobile," declared Mrs. Campbell. "Mrs. Andrews did not speak to either man. It was I who addressed the inquiry about how to get into the Rice and Hutchins' factory. But I spoke to the man standing in the rear of the car, not to the man underneath."

Why did Mrs. Andrews faint in court? Harry Kurlansky, a Quincy tailor, testified that she told him she fainted because the defense was digging into her past history, and that she was afraid the lawyers would "bring out the trouble she had with Mr. Landers." Landers was a naval officer, Kurlansky said.

She told him also, Kurlansky stated, that she couldn't identify the men at Braintree. The police wanted her to identify some one in Dedham jail as one of the men she saw in Braintree, but she couldn't because she didn't get a good look at the faces of those men. Kurlansky volunteered to testify for the defense after reading in newspapers of the "identification" she swore to in court.

Policeman George Fay of Quincy testified that he interviewed Mrs. Andrews in February, 1920, in connection with the alleged assault upon her. Did she suppose that attack had anything to do with the South Braintree affair? She answered that she could not identify the men she saw in Braintree as she didn't get a good look at them.

Alfred La Brecque, Quincy reporter and secretary of the Chamber of Commerce there, said she told him the same thing.

Miss Lena Allen, rooming house proprietor, testified that Mrs. Andrews' reputation for truth and veracity was bad, and that she would never want her in her house again.

At the end of the trial the Government put Mrs. Mary Gaines upon the stand to support the testimony of Mrs. Andrews and to contradict that of Mrs. Campbell. Mrs. Gaines declared that a few weeks after the crime she had heard Mrs. Andrews say in Mrs. Campbell's presence that she had spoken to the man under the automobile, and that Mrs. Campbell did not contradict her.

Fred Loring, shoe-worker for Slater and Morrill, stated that he found a dark brown cap near Berardelli's body; it was offered as an exhibit by the commonwealth. When tried on by Sacco on the witness stand this cap seemed too small; whereas a cap of his own, tried on immediately afterwards fitted with nicety.

The "bandit cap" was fur-lined and had ear-laps, which accounts for its being smaller although the same size numerically as Sacco's. Sacco never owned a cap of this character. George Kelley, superintendent of the Three K Factory where Sacco worked, said the cap he had seen daily behind Sacco's bench, as he remembered, was a pepper-and-salt cloth, which he believed was different from the one produced by the commonwealth. A cap like the one described by Kelley was found in the house at the time of Sacco's arrest.

Of the four bullets found in Berardelli's dead body, three were admittedly from a Savage pistol. The other one, however, was from some other kind of revolver, the make of which is in dispute. It is the prosecution's contention that the leaden pellet designated as Bullet No. 3 which inflicted the fatal wound upon Berardelli, was from a Colt automatic found on Sacco when he was arrested three weeks after the murders. The bullet was a Winchester of an obsolete make.

The testimony upon this point by experts put upon the stand by both the government and the defense was voluminous and highly technical. The disagreement was sharp.

Captain Charles Van Amburgh, of the Remington Arms Works, testified for the prosecution: "I believe the bullet was fired from a Colt automatic pistol... I am inclined to believe it was fired from this Colt automatic." He based this belief, he said, on a mark he found on the bullet, visible only under a microscope, and on similar marks noted on three bullets which he had fired from the revolver. These bullets were all Winchesters of a modern make. On three Peters bullets fired at the same time no such marks were visible. The Peters bullet, he said, are a trifle smaller than Winchesters, and therefore under less pressure. Under cross-examination, Van Amburg acknowledged that pitting such as was present in the Sacco pistol was generally caused by rust or fouling and that to the best of his judgment, in the pistol before them, it was so caused.

Captain William H. Proctor, head of the state police.

He said that bullet No. 3 was consistent with being fired from Sacco's revolver. "That bullet was fired from a 32 Colt automatic," Proctor asserted. "It has a left twist and a .060 of an inch groove. No other revolver except the Colt has a left twist."

"Don't you know," asked Defense Counsel McAnarney, "that at least two other kinds of revolvers make a left twist marking?"

"No, I don't," replied Proctor.

"Do you know that the Spear and the Sauer guns both make a left twist marking?"

Proctor didn't know. He had never seen either kind of gun, never heard of them before. Both are German makes, it appears, and occasionally one of them bobs up in a pawnshop.

Although this witness had said he had been a gun expert in a hundred cases, he was unable to take a Colt automatic revolver apart in court. Proctor struggled with it vainly until his face grew crimson, dropped it on the floor in his awkwardness, and then the court suggested that some one else try. Another expert took the weapon apart in a moment.

"And what is the part of the gun through which the firing pin protrudes," asked Attorney McAnarney.

"I do not know as I can tell you all the scientific parts of the gun," answered Proctor.

Proctor said he received the Colt pistol and some 32-calibre cartridges from another officer at Brockton police station.

Q. Will you look at this envelope of cartridges and see if you can identify them?

A. That is the same envelope, and it looks like the same amount of cartridges. I can tell by counting them.

Neither revolver nor the bullets were ever impounded before the trial. They were in the hands of police officers, and most of the time in Captain Proctor's possession. Prosecutor Katzmann refused to permit the defense to examine any of the exhibits until they were produced in court.

To meet the testimony of Proctor and Van Amburgh, the defense put on two gun experts of long standing—James E. Burns, noted rifleman, champion pistol shot, and head of a department of the United States Cartridge Company; and James H. Fitzgerald, superintendent of the testing department of the Colt Automatic Pistol Company. Burns declared that Bullet No. 3 might have been fired from either a Colt or a Bayard revolver. The latter is a Belgian gun; many have been brought here since the war. Burns declared positively that the bullet did not come from Sacco's revolver. He fired 8 bullets through it, and all came through clean and without any markings.

Fitzgerald testified that Bullet No. 3 did not come from the Sacco gun; that there was no condition existent in that gun to cause the peculiar marking on the bullet.

Expert Burns fired U. S. bullets, for the reason that, as stated above, the "fatal" bullet was of an obsolete make, and he had found it impossible to secure an exact duplicate in spite of having made great effort to do so. He considered that the U. S. bullets which he used corresponded more nearly with the "fatal" bullet than did the newer make of Winchester used by Captain Van Amburgh.

To the minds of many who followed this gun testimony, the claim of the government regarding a certain gun seemed farcical. The fact that two of the bullets said to have been fired through the so-called Sacco gun did bear microscopic marks faintly resembling that on the "fatal bullet" seems to have carried weight with some members of the jury; that is indicated by the circumstance that the microscope was called for while the verdict was under consideration. The question was so involved, the chances of error so great, the opinion of experts so conflicting, that it would seem as if a layman could hardly have made a final judgment on the matter.

Then came up the testimony about Sacco's reputation.

From 1910 to 1917 he worked in the Milford Shoe Factory. The foreman during four years of this time, John J. Millick, a responsible looking person of the English operative type, testified of Sacco, "a steady workman, never lost a day." Asked as to his reputation as a peaceful and law-abiding citizen, he answered "good."

Michael F. Kelley, the senior partner in the Three K Factory at Stoughton where Sacco was employed the 18 months previous to his arrest, and his son George Kelley, superintendent and part owner, bore testimony as to Sacco's character similar to that of Mr. Millick.

Both of the Kelleys gave testimony which dovetailed in with that of others in establishing Sacco's alibi. Late in March, Sacco had told both Michael and George Kelley that he had received letters from Italy announcing his mother's death, and that he must go home as soon as possible to see his father. With George Kelley he had arranged to break in another man to do his work and that he should be free to start for Italy as soon as his place was satisfactorily filled.

On Monday or Tuesday of the week of April 15th, Sacco told George Kelley he would like a day off that week, to make a trip to Boston and get the passport. On Wednesday, April 14th, Sacco told him that he was well ahead of his work and would go to Boston the following day. He was absent the following day, Thursday, April 15th (the fateful day of the South Braintree murder), in Boston; so Sacco claimed and so George Kelley believed. The day following that, April 16th, Sacco was at work at the usual hour. This day, the 15th of April, was the only day of absence which George Kelley recalled. And he believed he would have remembered had Sacco been absent on any other day as his was "a one-man job," and if "he was out, the work was blocked."

It was not controverted that Sacco had been to Boston about his passport at approximately the date he claimed. Whether he had really gone to Boston on April 15th as he claimed, or to South Braintree to commit murder as the Government claimed, was the issue of the trial. Ten witnesses supported the alibi. The truthfulness of their testimony was not impeached, although efforts were made to impeach the reliability of their memory. However, it appears that they certainly saw Sacco in various parts of Boston some day that week. And since Thursday was the only day it was shown that Sacco was not at work, the conclusion is obvious.

Mrs. Sacco, when upon the witness stand, unwittingly to herself buttressed her husband's alibi claim. She fixed the date he had gone for the passport by the visit she received from a friend who had come with his wife from Milford the day her husband was absent, and who had stayed to dinner. The friend she said was Enrico Iacovelli whom her husband had sent for to see Mr. Kelley and arrange to be broken into Sacco's work.

Henry Iacovelli, the shoe-worker who took Sacco's place in the Kelley factory, testified that he received a letter from Mr. Kelley offering him Sacco's job as an edge-trimmer, a highly important function in the factory mechanism. He replied that he could go and talk with Kelley on April 15; went to see him that day; called at the Sacco home to see Sacco; Mrs. Sacco informed him that her husband was in Boston arranging for passports.

The original correspondence exchanged between Kelley and Iacovelli was introduced as evidence by the defense.

Sacco declared under oath that he took the 8:56 o'clock train from South Stoughton to Boston on April 15, to arrange for passports to Italy. South Stoughton is 19 miles from Boston.

In Boston, Sacco said, he had lunch with friends at Boni's restaurant in North Square, then went to the Italian consulate to see about the passports. A photograph of his wife, his son Dante and himself which he brought was too large for consular purposes; there was considerable conversation about that; he was instructed to furnish a smaller picture.

On the streets he met and talked with certain persons. Going again to North Square, he spent some time in Giordano's coffee-house; then went to East Boston, where he paid a bill for groceries, and finally returned to Stoughton on a train about 4:20 p. m.

Prof. Felice Guadagni, journalist and lecturer, testified that he had lunch at Boni's on April 15 with Sacco and Albert Bosco, editor of *La Notizia*. While they ate, John D. Williams, an advertising agent, entered and joined them. Sacco told them about his intention to visit the consulate. They discussed the banquet given that day by Italians to Mr. Williams of the *Boston Transcript* who had been decorated by the King of Italy for the stand his paper had taken in the war—a memorable occasion among Boston Italians.

Later that afternoon Guadagni met Sacco again in Giordano's coffee-house. And after the arrest of the defendants, Guadagni said he visited the consulate and talked with Giuseppe Adrower, clerk there, establishing the fact that Sacco had applied for a passport on April 15 and had been sent away because the photograph he brought was too large.

Prof. Antonio Dentamaro, Manager of the Foreign Department of the Haymarket National Bank in Boston, testified in court that he met Sacco in Giordano's coffee-house on April 15, between 2 and 3 p. m. Remembered date because he went to the Coffee House directly from the banquet to Mr. Williams which he had attended.

He especially remembered meeting Sacco because he had sent a message by him to Leone Mucci, a member of the Chamber of Deputies in Italy.

They had talked about Sacco's prospective return to Italy. Sacco had said he had come to Boston to get his passport.

Albert Bosco, editor of *La Notizia,* conservative Italian daily newspaper in Boston, testified likewise as to the presence of Sacco and the others in Boni's on that day.

Carlo Affè, East Boston grocer, testified that between 3 and 4 o'clock on April 15 he was paid by Sacco for an order of groceries purchased at an earlier date. He exhibited a notebook record of the transaction.

Giuseppe Adrower, clerk in the Italian consulate at Boston for 6 years, and now in Italy, testified in a deposition sworn to before the American consul general at Rome. He identified the photograph of Sacco, Mrs. Sacco and their son as a picture Sacco brought to the consulate on April 15. He corroborated Sacco's statements regarding his difficulties over passports.

Adrower remembered telling Sacco that the picture was too large, and that he laughed with others in the consulate over the big photograph, and his eye happened to catch the date on the calendar while so doing. Sacco left the consulate a few minutes before the office was closed for the day; it is regularly open from 10 to 3. Very few persons were there that afternoon... Adrower went to Italy May 20, for his health, but Guadagni testified that he talked with Adrower about Sacco and the photograph shortly after Sacco's arrest.

One alibi witness who was brought forward late in the trial and by the merest chance offered what would seem to be incontrovertible evidence. It appeared that Sacco one day had noticed a face in the audience at the court-room which arrested his attention. He called for Mr. McAnarney and asked him to find out if that man was on the train coming from Boston to Stoughton in the evening of April 15, 1920. Mr. McAnarney called the man into the lobby and inquired. "I don't know," answered the stranger, "but will see if I can find out."

It developed that he was a contractor who kept his own time in his business books, by the hour; and from his books put in evidence and from a check dated April 15th, and used to buy supplies in Boston upon the date in question as well as by the bills for these supplies, he was able to locate himself on that very train. He did not know Sacco and had no recollection of having ever seen him until he dropped in as a spectator at the trial. His name is James M. Hayes; his residence and place of business, Stoughton, Mass.

The District Attorney, attempting to demolish Sacco's alibi in his closing argument, was silent as to the evidence offered by Hayes.

TESTIMONY RELATING TO BOTH— AND TO NEITHER

The discussion of the testimony against Vanzetti and against Sacco must be supplemented with a number of other considerations. In the first place, there were 22 persons on the stand for the defense on the issue of identifications, who had at least as good an opportunity to see the crime and the criminals as the several state witnesses, and who said positively that these were not the bandits.

In the second place, 13 witnesses put on the stand by the

prosecution for the purpose of establishing some facts of the crime, of whom several were excellently placed to make identifications, and certainly seemed anxious to apprehend the guilty persons, could not identify either of the defendants.

Thirdly, the government sought to bolster its testimony by evolving a far-fetched and intangible theory of "consciousness of guilt" at the time of arrest, which in turn brought into the limelight the circumstances of the arrest and the defendants' unpopular social views. There are also a number of other points which consumed much time, clouded the issues, and really had no bearing upon the case.

Testimony contradicting that of Mary Eva Splaine and Frances Devlin was given by Frank Burke, lecturer, who observed the bandits escape from a much better vantage point than either woman. He was on Pearl street near the New Haven tracks and in the immediate path of the escaping car.

He stood within ten feet of the automobile. He saw two men in it, both dark. The bandit leaning out of the rear seat pointed an automatic pistol at him and pulled the trigger, but there was no explosion. Burke got a full view of the man who the prosecution claimed was Sacco. He described him as very full-faced—flat, and a broad, heavy jaw; needed a shave badly, "dark complexioned, looked rather a desperate type of man."

But Burke declared that neither bandit was Sacco nor Vanzetti. He had an unobstructed view of the car as it fled, while the view of Miss Splaine and Miss Devlin was cut off by the cobbler shop. From a distance of ten feet instead of 80 as in the case of Misses Splaine and Devlin he described the man on the right side front seat who the government claims was Sacco.

Winfred Pierce and Laurence Ferguson, shoe-workers on third floor of Hampton House, saw bandit-car escape from a window directly above where Miss Splaine and Miss Devlin observed the car. Pierce saw one bandit shoot at his friend, Carl Knipps. Both described the bandit leaning out of the car and shooting, but declared neither Sacco nor Vanzetti was that man.

Barbara Liscomb, a woman of about thirty, of good personality, employed as a heeler, on the third floor of the Rice and

Hutchins factory.   She looked from a window directly above
the room in which Pelser 'worked.   She had heard shots, ran to
the window; saw two men lying on the ground; a dark man with
a pistol in hand standing over Berardelli.   He wheeled around
and pointed the pistol at her.   She fainted, but in the instant of
observation, she declared the image of the bandit was firmly
implanted in her mind.   "I shall remember that face all my life.
That man was neither of the defendants.   Of that I am positive."

Mrs. Jennie Novelli, trained nurse, saw a big touring car
drive slowly up the street shortly before the murder occurred
and took particular notice of the chauffeur and the man beside
him, whom she thought at first she recognized.   Asked if either
of these men were Sacco or Vanzetti she answered, "No, they
were not."

Albert Frantello, worker in Slater and Morrill plant.
Passed from one factory building to another at 2:55 p. m.   Saw
two men leaning on fence in front of Rice and Hutchins factory.
Was close enough to touch them.   Frantello, who is American of
Italian descent, is certain Sacco and Vanzetti are not those two
men.   Was interviewed by state police officers, and was not
summoned by prosecution.

One of the men whom Frantello described was the bandit
with whom it was sought to identify Sacco.

Daniel J. O'Neil, 19 years old, a business school graduate,
got off the train from Boston and was sitting in a taxi-cab with
a Mr. Gilman when he heard the shooting.   He got a distinct
impression of at least one of the bandits at a distance of 155 to
170 feet from the automobile.   He said positively that neither
of the defendants was the man he saw.

Five among 22 defense witnesses were laborers shoveling in
an excavation across the street from the shooting.   They were
foreigners who had to speak through interpreters.   In cross-
examination it was sought to show that they had been too scared
or too far from the scene of action to see anything.   Their
testimony was not broken down, but presumably was accorded
little weight.   One of them, a Spaniard by the name of Pedro
Iscorla, was 40 or 50 feet from crime-action; had gone to get
a drink of water.   Says man who shot policeman (that is Berar-

delli) was high and thin, slim. Light complexion, 5 feet 8 or 9. Man who shot paymaster was a little˙shorter and dark.

Emilio Falcone, was a hundred feet from crime-action. Saw man who did shooting; he was light, tall. Not Sacco nor Vanzetti. Henry Cerro, granite-cutter from Vermont, also worked in excavation. Saw shooting 90 feet away. Parmenter was shot by a light-haired man, he declared.

Five other witnesses were working on the railroad some distance from the crossing and claimed to have run up toward the gate house in time to see the bandit-car cross the track. Angelo Ricci, section gang foreman was put on later by the government to show that they had not left the place where they were at work. Under cross-examination he had exclaimed, "What the hell, I did the best I could; when you've got 24 men you can't put a string on them. I told them to stop and if they sneaked around the piles of dirt I couldn't help it." One of these laborers, Joseph Cellucci, wearing the uniform of a sailor from the training station at Newport News, declared he stood within 10 or 12 feet of the car, and that one of the bandits fired a shot at him which left him deaf for 3 days. He described that man and another sitting beside the driver; both about 20 years old. Neither one was Sacco nor Vanzetti, he declared.

Another of them, Nicola Gatti, is especially important because he had been a neighbor of Sacco in Milford eight years back. Had he seen him in the bandit car he could not have failed to remember. Said he got a good view of the two men in front (with one of them it was sought to identify Sacco) and one behind. Asked if either of the defendants were any of these men, he answered, "No."

Thirteen prosecution witnesses testified to facts pertinent to the exact moment of the murders, or in connection with the escape—but did not identify. Of these, several could not have been expected to make identification, but others had an excellent view. Five of these have already been discussed under Sacco's case because they were in a position to see the bandit whom the government sought to identify with Sacco. The others are Shelley Neal, Mrs. Annie Nichols, Harris A. Colbert, Daniel

Buckley, Mrs. Alta Baker, F. C. Clark, John P. Lloyd, and Julia Kelliher.

Neal was an important government witness because he attempted to identify the bandit-car with an automobile stationed against the entrance of the express office, in the morning when the money arrived. He claims to have seen neither Sacco nor Vanzetti.

A summary of the identification testimony for the government and for the defense is now in place. Of 35 witnesses called, 7 were unable to make any identifications; 22 were certain that neither Sacco nor Vanzetti were the men they had seen; 4 identified Sacco—two of them making serious changes from former testimony, and the other two thoroughly discredited; only one, the man whom the prosecution itself was obliged to "interpret," identified Vanzetti.

The prosecution contended that the defendants, by their action, attitude and utterances on the night of May 5, when they where arrested, displayed consciousness of guilt of the South Braintree murders.

Officer Michael Connolly who arrested Sacco and Vanzetti in a trolley car going into Brockton, asserts that as he approached them Vanzetti put his hand in his hip pocket and that thereupon he, Connolly, said: "You keep your hands in your lap or you will be sorry." Connolly further testified that a revolver was taken off Vanzetti by Officer Vaughn, who boarded the car at the next station, and that he, Connolly kept him covered until he delivered him at the police station. This story Vanzetti absolutely contradicted. With officer Connolly making the arrest was officer Vaughn. Vaughn said he took the revolver from Vanzetti's right hip pocket (Transcript, p. 1280). Connolly said it was in left (Transcript p. 1284).

In the automobile which carried the arrested men to police station, Connolly testified that Sacco twice reached his hand to put it under his overcoat, and that he told him to keep his hand outside his clothes and on his lap. That some conversation about keeping hands where they belong may have taken place is confirmed by Officer Merle A. Spear, driving the automobile, who testified to hearing Sacco say, "You needn't be afraid of me."

The government drew from this testimony a deduction of "consciousness of guilt." What, they ask, could have prompted men to resist arrest, unless there was a murder on their conscience?

"The consciousness of guilt" made so much of by Judge Thayer was the consciousness of the dead body of their comrade Salsedo lying smashed in the spring dawn two days before on the pavement of Park Row.

XI

AFTER THE TRIAL

Since the conviction of Sacco and Vanzetti on July 14th 1921, that shocked a large part of humanity as has no legal decision since Dreyfus was sent to Devil's Island, the Defense Committee, backed up by contributions from all over the United States and from every part of the world where a labor movement exists has managed so far to stave off the sentence. The motion for a new trial that has just been denied was the seventh; first under Fred H. Moore and later under William G. Thompson, an eminent Boston attorney, president of a committee of the Massachusetts Bar Association, who has had the courage and sense of duty as a citizens to take up vigorously and at the risk of loss of practice and friends an unpopular cause. It is largely due to Mr. Thompson's personal influence and his general reputation for conservatism and integrity that lawyers and ministers and college professors and newspaper readers generally are becoming interested in the case. Now that the *Boston Herald* has come out editorially for a new trial, and suggested the appointment of an unprejudiced commission to review the whole course of the case, there is growing, if belated, agitation in liberal and intellectual circles. The people of Massachusetts are beginning to get an inkling of the fact that in so grave a miscarriage of justice there is more at stake than the lives of two Italian radicals.

The first motion for a retrial argued in October 1921 was based on the claim that the verdict was not in accord with the evidence. It was denied.

Four more motions were based on newly discovered evidence. The first charged irregularities in the jury room. The foreman of the jury, Ripley, a former Chief of Police of Quincy, who must have carried great weight with his fellow jurors, stated to the defense that he had in his pockets at the trial some cartridges of similar make and calibre to some of those in evidence, and that there was some discussion between him and other jurors about them. Presumably they were used for purposes of comparison and inference. At all events such secret evidence directly violates the conception of due process of law, which insists that a man shall have the opportunity to subject to the test of cross-examination all evidence offered against him. A friend of Ripley's also gave an affidavit to the effect that Ripley, before the trial and knowing he was to sit on the jury, said to him, "Damn them, (Sacco and Vanzetti), they ought to hang them, anyway."

The motion was denied.

The second motion for a new trial was based on the testimony of Louis Pelzer. Prior to the trial, according to the defense's affidavits, Pelzer said that he witnessed the shooting of the paymaster and his guard. He saw a wounded man sink into the roadway, and because the bullets were firing toward the window of the Rice & Hutchins factory, where he worked, he dropped under a bench and did not move until the bandit car crossed the railroad tracks 500 feet away. At least, this was his story to an investigator for the defense.

On the witness stand, however, Pelzer made a positive identification of Sacco as one of the bandits. On cross-examination he said he had lied to the defense's investigators. Four months afterward he signed a long affidavit saying that his original statement was true, that the testimony he gave at the trial was untrue and that he gave it because he was coerced by the District Attorney. In his affidavit he asserted that the words: "He (Sacco) is the dead image" of the bandit were put into his mouth by the District Attorney.

Six months later Pelser recanted his recantation in a statement to the District Attorney. This time he said his statement to the defense's investigator was untrue, that his trial testimony was true, that the statement made after trial was untrue and the last statement to the District Attorney true.

In connection with the second motion the defense filed an affidavit sworn to by Roy E. Gould, an itinerant vendor of razor paste, who alleges that the bandit on the right-hand side of the fleeing car fired at him and that a bullet went through his coat. He was arrested by the police, but was released when he convinced them of his innocence. He told the officers that he would be able to identify the bandits, and gave them his name and address. The prosecution did not call Gould. Through the mention of his name in a newspaper article the defense, after laborious search through half a dozen States, found him at Portland, Me., eight months after the trial. He was confronted with the convicted men and swore that they were not the bandits he saw on the day of the shooting. Motion denied.

The defense, in its third motion for a new trial, produced affidavits to show that Carlos E. Goodridge, one of the prosecution's important witnesses, had a criminal record in several States. At the trial Goodridge said he rushed out of a poolroom on hearing the shots, observed the bandit car whizzing by and saw Sacco in the front seat, and that Sacco tried to shoot him.

It so happened that some months before the trial one of the defense counsel had been instrumental in prosecuting Goodridge on a charge of having stolen a victrola. The news of the arrest of Sacco and Vanzetti on May 5, 1920, was followed by the visit to the jail of many who said they had seen the bandits. Goodridge, the defense asserted, did not go. However, he was taken to court to plead guilty on the same day that Sacco and Vanzetti were taken to court. Subsequently he told the prosecution that he recognized the two Italians and was let out on probation .

The affidavits of Goodridge's life presented by the defense cover 160 pages. His real name was stated to be Erastus Corning Whitney. He is said to have been convicted in New York of grand larceny before reaching his twentyfirst year. After serving a three-year sentence he received his freedom and a year later was again arrested for stealing a relative's jewelry. His second conviction was for a term of three years. Upon his release he began stealing horses. He was indicted for stealing a horse and buggy. The affidavits signed by District Attorneys, sheriffs, ministers and others declared that Goodridge's reputation for veracity was bad, that he was a petty thief, a swindler of women, and a confidence man. Motion denied.

The fourth motion for a new trial was concerned with the testimony of Lola R. Andrews. According to the defense's affidavits Mrs. Andrews was interviewed by them five months before the trial. She said she did not see Sacco, and her description of the man she saw, according to the defense, was not that of Sacco. "He is not the man," she said upon seeing photographs of Sacco. The night before she was called by the Commonwealth she told defense counsel that she did not know why she was being called as she could not identify anybody.

Next day she made a positive identification of Sacco. Cross-examined on the stenographic notes of her conversation with defense counsel she said the stenographer had not transcribed his notes honestly. She branded as a lie the statement made by the lawyer for the defense. During her cross-examination she fainted three times and was assisted from the room.

In an affidavit sworn to by Mrs. Andrews nine months after the trial she declared that her original statement before trial was true, and that her trial testimony was untrue and had been given under the coercion and intimidation of the District Attorney's office, which threatened to reveal her private life.

(Six months later Mrs. Andrews, in a statement to the District Attorney's office, said that her first statement to the defense lawyer was false, her trial testimony true, her subsequent affidavit to the defense counsel untrue and her last statement true). Motion denied.

The fifth motion for a new trial was concerned with the exceedingly important gun-and-bullet testimony. The Commonwealth held that the bullet that killed Berardelli was fired from Sacco's pistol. Two gun experts for the defense said it was not.

The Commonwealth's experts were Captain Charles A. Van Amburgh of the Remington Arms Works and Captain William H. Proctor, for thirty years head of the Massachusetts State Police.

According to the new evidence placed before the court, Captain Proctor states that he had the death bullet and the Sacco pistol in his possession for more than a year before the trial and that with Mr. Van Amburgh he conducted certain tests with Sacco's pistol. In his affidavit, made on Oct. 22, 1923, more than two and a half years after the trial, Captain Proctor stated that at the trial and at the moment of making the affidavit he was entirely unconvinced that the mortal bullet had passed through Sacco's pistol. He said:

"At no time was I able to find any evidence whatever which tended to convince me that the particular mortal bullet found in Berardelli's body, which came from a Colt automatic pistol, which I think was numbered 3 and had some other exibit number, came from Sacco's pistol, and I so informed the District Attorney and his assistants before the trial.

"This bullet was what is commonly called a full metal patch bullet, and, although I repeatedly talked over with Captain Van Amburg the scratch or scratches which he claimed tended to indentify this bullet as one that must have gone through Sacco's pistol, his statements concerning the indentifying marks seemed to me entirely unconvincing.

"At the trial the District Atorney did not ask me whether I had found any evidence that the so-called mortal bullet, which I have referred to as number 3, passed through Sacco's pistol, nor was I asked that question in cross-examination. The District Attorney desired to ask me that question, but I had repeatedly told him that if he did I should be obliged to answer in the negative; consequently he put to me this question:

"Q. 'Have you an opinion as to whether bullet number 3 was fired from the Colt automatic which is in evidence?' To which I answered, 'I have'.

"He then proceeded, Q. 'And what is your opinion?' A. 'My opinion is that it is consistent with being fired by that pistol.'

"That is still my opinion, for the reason that bullet number 3, in my judgment, passed through some Colt automatic pistol; but 1 do not intend by that answer to imply that the so-called mortal bullet had passed through this particular Colt automatic pistol, and the District Attorney well knew that I did not so intend, and framed his question accordingly. Had I been asked the direct question, whether I found any affirmative evidence whatever that this so-called mortal bullet had passed through this particular Sacco's pistol, I should have answered then, as I do now, without hesitation, in the negative."

Frederick G. Katzmann, who was District Attorney at the time of the trial, and Harold P. Williams, later his successor, filed affidavits on this motion. Mr. Katzmann stated that Captain Proctor told him that it was his opinion that the mortal bullet had been fired from "a" Colt automatic pistol. He did not say that it had been fired from Sacco's pistol. Mr. Williams said that Captain Proctor could not tell through what pistol the mortal bullet had been fired. He also denied that Captain Proctor's attention had been "repeatedly" called to the question whether he could find any evidence which would justify the opinion that the death bullet came from the Sacco pistol.

In a sense the gun-and-bullet testimony is the crux of the case, for Judge Thayer, in his charge to the jury, said in substance that the jurors should consider Captain Proctor's testimony that the death bullet passed through Sacco's pistol. In his summary the District Attorney said to the jury, "You might disregard all the identification testimony and base your verdict on the testimony of these experts."

Additional new evidence to prove that the death bullet could not have been fired from Sacco's pistol was furnished to the court in the micro-photographs made by Albert H. Hamilton, who has offered expert testimony in many murder trials in which photographs taken under a compound microscope have been placed in evidence.

Taking the mortal bullet and test bullets fired through Sacco's pistol, Mr. Hamilton pointed out several markings in the mortal bullet which he said did not appear in those that were fired as a test. The prosecution sought to show many similarities in the marking of both exhibits.

Photographs of Mr. Hamilton showed that the shell which the Commonwealth claimed had been fired from Sacco's pistol had a dent in the exact centre where the firing pin struck it. The test shells, it was said, had dents 23 degrees off centre. The prosecution urged that both were so nearly in the middle as to make it certain that all had been fired from the same pistol.

There followed the appeal to the Supreme Judicial Court in January 1926. Despite a masterly argument by counsel for the defense the appeal was unanimously denied.

Meanwhile new evidence had been discovered, the affidavits of Letherman and Weyand tended to prove the contention of the defense that their radicalism had been a deciding factor in these men's conviction. The confession of Madeiros and the circumstantial case erected by the defense tending to prove that the South Braintree crime had been committed by the Morelli gang of Providence (a case that though circumstantial seems to a layman infinitely better founded than the state's case against Sacco and Vanzetti) gave the friends of Sacco and Vanzetti fresh hope that at last a new trial would be granted. The motions were denied.

Now there is only the growing force of public opinion between Sacco and Vanzetti and the electric chair. A new appeal to the Supreme Judicial Court is being prepared, but it seems hardly likely that the court will reverse its firmly-entrenched decision. There remains the faint hope of an appeal to the Supreme Court of the United States on the plea that the men were convicted without due process of law.

Will the people of this country and the citizens of Massachusetts stand by and see two men murdered by the dead weight of legal technicalities? Madeiros, murderer and gunman, was granted a second trial, on the plea that the judge had neglected to inform the jury that they should deem a man innocent until he was proven guilty. It is hard for anyone not versed in subtleties of the law to see why the same thing should not apply to Sacco and Vanzetti. The words were probably pronounced solemnly enough, but can anyone who has read over the account of the trial solemnly affirm that the spirit was there?

"So you left Plymouth to dodge the draft, did you?" was Katzmann's first question to Vanzetti on the stand. "Did you love your country in the last week of May, 1917? Is your love for the United States commensurate with the amount of money you can get in this country per week? Did you intend to condemn Harvard College?" were some of the questions put to Sacco—many of them really invitations to an argument. And Sacco was induced, and allowed by the judge, to make a long speech on his offensive political opinions. Katzmann's address to the jury ended with the words "stand together, you men of Norfolk County!" And Judge Thayer's charge opened as follows: "Gentlemen of the Jury, the Commonwealth of Massachusetts called upon you to render a most important service. Although you knew that such service would be arduous, painful and tiresome, yet you, like the true soldier, responded to that call in the spirit of supreme American loyalty." After three pages of this, he proceeds: "Having cleared away any mist of sympathy or prejudice from your minds and having substituted there trust, a purer atmosphere of unyielding impartiality and absolute fairness, let us take up some of the rights granted by law to the defendants...."

The men of Norfolk County stood together as best they knew, to defend their institutions against reds, slackers, foreign agitators. Twelve doughboys trying a German spy would have brought the same verdict. "Damn them, they ought to hang them anyway" was the foreman's opinion.

That was the history of the case from the outside. What was happening to the two men in jail? Hope and despair in sickening alternations, and then at last a sort of numbness. They, each of them, had moments of breakdown. At one time Vanzetti was put in a cell near the heating plant in Charlestown jail from which he could hear the hammering of men getting the electric chair ready for an execution. It wore on his nerves until the prison authorities became alarmed and sent him to the State Asylum for observation. There he was found to be perfectly sane.

But Vanzetti serving out his sentence at Charlestown, at least has work to keep him busy. In Dedham jail there is no provision for giving work to prisoners awaiting sentence. Except for the daily hour of exercise, Sacco has spent the whole six years shut up in a cell. At first he used to go through all sorts of exercises to keep himself fit; but inevitably the hopelessness of it got to him. He went on a hunger strike. After thirty-one days he was removed, a wreck, to the State Farm at Bridgewater. There he was allowed to do outside work. Once he was well he was moved back to Dedham again for more days and weeks and months of waiting. The thing that keeps these two men alive and sane is their faith in themselves as champions, martyrs of the working class. Vanzetti is very fond of the phrase of St. Augustine. *The blood of martyrs is the seed of liberty.*

For through the bars and walls of their jails these men must have felt an inkling of the great heroic shadows they throw on the minds of working men all over the world. In Russia, in Germany, in France, in the Argentine, people have been profoundly moved by every step in the case. There have been meetings, parades, bombs thrown, heads broken for Sacco and Vanzetti, among men whose languages they may never know, the names of whose towns they never heard. History is made up of these sudden searchlights that for a moment make gigantic the drama of a single humble man.

The tangible proof of this feeling is in the contributions that pour in steadily to the Defense Committee, mostly collected from poor people, in small sums, from people to whom giving up a dollar or two means missing meals or cigarettes or moving picture shows. In the month of June 1926 contributions came in from Chicago, Newark, Pensacola, Fla., Kalispell, Mont., Baltimore, Bound Rock, N. J., Bass River, Mass., New York, Buffalo, Boston, Sandusky, Detroit, Zanesville, O., San Diego, Oshkosh, Tulsa, London, England, Pueblo, Colo., Coney Island, Balboa, San Francisco... and a couple of hundred other places. Whatever the outcome, the passionate effort evoked by this case will have been a great proof, if not of working class strength, at least of working class solidarity.

With the backing of the Italian population of the towns round Boston and of a few liberal-minded Americans of old families who had enough imagination and good citizenship to see that justice was dangerously miscarrying, the Defense Committee has carried on the case. They have been gravely hampered by a lack of knowledge of American customs, and by the dircet action of certain underground forces. There were found to be undercover men working as collectors. Frank R. Lopez, an active member of the Committee, was deported to Spain. Then there was the still unsolved De Falco case.

One morning in January 1921 a certain Angelina De Falco, who claimed to be a court interpreter at Dedham, called at the office of the Defense Committee accompanied by a certain Cicchetti of Providence and offered to get Sacco off in the trial that was to come. After several meetings during which the woman tried to gain the confidence of Felicani and Guadagni, two of the members of the Committee, she declared herself to be an emissary of District Attorney Katzmann and of the clerk of the court at Dedham. More meetings in restaurants and cafes. At length she made them believe that for a certain sum of money she could get off both Sacco and Vanzetti. But at the next interview she came back to her original statement that she could only get Sacco off; Vanzetti was too difficult on account of the previous conviction. Then Guadagni said there was nothing doing. The committee was out to prove the innocence of both men. She said that it would cost a great deal; the District Attorney and his assistants and the foreman of the jury would all have to be fixed; there would be a mock trial and the two men would be acquitted. The morning of January 5th Mrs. De Falco telephoned the Committee, presumably from Dedham, that everything was O. K. The seventh they were supposed to go to Dedham to settle the matter.

The lawyers for the defense, fearing a trap, suggested that Mrs. De Falco be invited to discuss terms in Boston instead of in Dedham. A good deal annoyed she came into the office at 32 Battery Street. A dictaphone had been put in to register the conversation. There in the presence of Felicani, Guadagni, Mrs. Sproul and Orciani she repeated her proposition. The price of the two men's liberty was forty thousand dollars. It was explained to her that they had no such sum on hand. She said that if an advance of five thousand was paid, the case would be adjourned till the autumn session in order to give the Committee all summer to raise the money.

"And if the money is not raised will they be convicted?" asked Mrs. Sproul and Guadagni. "Certainly", replied Angelina

De Falco. Negotiations dragged on. Chief Counsel Moore was of the opinion that they ought to swear out a complaint and have her arrested. They did so. The case was tried before Judge Francis Murray in Boston, who dismissed the charges, completely exonerating Mr. Katzmann, ruling that Mrs. De Falco had been 'indiscreet', but not guilty of a criminal act.

Of course Mrs. De Falco may simply have been trying to play a little game on her own, but the ugly doubt remains that there may have been more to it than that. If you turn back to the Boston papers of that period you will find that certain scandalous disclosures were being made as to the actions of the district attorneys of Suffolk and Middlesex counties.

Anyway that's the last that was heard of Angelina De Falco. The mystery is still unsolved.

What is going to be done if the Supreme Judicial Court continues to refuse Sacco and Vanzetti a new trial? Are Sacco and Vanzetti going to burn in the Chair?

The conscience of the people of Massachusetts must be awakened. Working people, underdogs, reds know instinctively what is going on. The same thing has happened before. But the average law-admiring, authority-respecting citizen does not know. For the first time, since Judge Thayer's last denial of motions for a new trial, there has been a certain awakening among the influential part of the community, the part of the community respected by the press and the bench and the pulpit. Always there have been notable exceptions, but up to now these good citizens have had no suspicion that anything but justice was being meted out by the courts. Goaded by the *New York World* editorials, by Chief Counsel Thompson's eloquence, by the *Boston Herald's* courageous change of front, they are getting uneasy. It remains to be seen what will come of this uneasiness. The *Boston Herald* suggests an impartial commission to review the whole case. All that is needed is that the facts of the case be generally known.

Everyone must work to that end, no matter what happens, that the facts of the case may be known so that no one can plead ignorance, so that if these men are killed, everyone in the

State, everyone in the country will have the guilt on them. So that no one can say "I would have protested but I didn't know what was being done."

Tell your friends, write to your congressmen, to the political bosses of your district, to the newspapers. Demand the truth about Sacco and Vanzetti. Call meetings, try to line up trade unions, organizations, clubs, put up posters. Demand the truth about Sacco and Vanzetti.

If the truth had been told they would be free men today.

If the truth is not told they will burn in the Chair in Charlestown Jail. If they die what little faith many millions of men have in the chance of Justice in this country will die with them.

Save Sacco and Vanzetti.